Peter Beyerhaus

MISSIONS: WHICH WAY?

HUMANIZATION OR REDEMPTION

Foreword by Donald McGavran
Preface by Harold Lindsell

Translated by MARGARET CLARKSON

ZONDERVAN PUBLISHING HOUSE
GRAND RAPIDS, MICHIGAN

MISSIONS — WHICH WAY?
© 1971 by Zondervan Publishing House
Grand Rapids, Michigan

Library of Congress Catalog Card Number 79-171195

Formerly published under the title
Humanisierung — Einzige Hoffnung Der Welt.

Quotations from the New English Bible are
© 1961, 1970 by the Delegates of the Oxford
University Press and the Syndics of the Cambridge
University Press, and are used by permission.

Printed in the United States of America

Contents

Foreword

The great issues in Christian mission are theological. The question is: What does God command the Church to do in regard to the multitudes who have no knowledge of Christ?

One of the most crucial aspects of the tremendous revolution now shaking the world and the Church is exactly this, that Christians answer that question in different ways. What is mission in the midst of the rapidly changing world? What is mission in the face of racial inequality, political oppression, and economic injustice? What is mission in the face of two billion who have never heard the name of the Savior?

Out of North America alone at least two hundred million dollars and thousands of missionaries will be committed one way or another according to convictions as to what mission *is* theologically and biblically.

Consequently, everyone who prays for and gives to missions should read this book. It was written for the German churches, but speaks significantly to the American situation also. In it, Dr. Peter Beyerhaus, the well-known professor of missions in Tübingen University in Germany, and one of the chief architects of the famed *Frankfurt Declaration,* bares the choices lying before the churches. He deals with profound issues clearly. When the Christian has read this terse book, he will know what the alternatives in mission today really are and *will be able to evaluate each in the white light of the biblical revelation.* No more important book on missions has been published in the last ten years.

DONALD MCGAVRAN
Dean, School of World Mission
and Institute of Church Growth

*Fuller Theological Seminary
Pasadena, California*

Preface

This book written by Professor Beyerhaus of the University of Tübingen was first published in German and brought to my attention by Dr. Donald McGavran of the School of World Mission at Fuller Theological Seminary in Pasadena, California. Before I saw the English translation of the manuscript I had come to know of the work of Professor Beyerhaus through the Frankfurt Declaration, which was published in the pages of *Christianity Today*. The book and the Declaration go hand in hand and should not be separated from each other.

At the time the Frankfurt Declaration was published in *Christianity Today* I stated that this document represented a breakthrough on the contemporary German scene. For fifteen German professors and a number of other people to sign such a declaration was amazing, particularly in the light of the theological situation in Germany for the last one hundred years. To understand both the book and the Declaration it is necessary to go back to Uppsala, Sweden, in 1968 when the fourth General Assembly of the World Council of Churches convened. At this time the ecumenical movement defined the task of evangelism to consist in changing the social, political, and economic structures. Humanism was increasingly in vogue among World Council members and some of the delegates tended more and more toward universalism and syncretism. The youth at Uppsala who did not have the right to vote represented a radicalized element of the younger generation whose interest was to push the World Council as far left of center as possible.

At Uppsala, the report of Section 2 of the General Assembly, having to do with the mission of the Church and the spread of the Gospel, was a focal point for discontent among evangelicals. The preliminary document for Section 2 which was issued prior to the Assembly meetings at Uppsala was less than satisfactory. Dr. Donald McGavran in his *Church Growth Bulletin* was highly critical of the pre-Assembly document, stating categorically that it left out of the ecumenical movement's consideration two billion people who had never heard or had not accepted the Gospel of Jesus Christ. At Uppsala, John R. W. Stott of All Souls Church in Langham Place, London, was successful in amending parts of Section 2. Unfortunately, when the document emerged it was internally inconsistent, for the inclusion of the material suggested by Mr. Stott struck a note that was foreign to the remainder of the material of that document.

When Professor Beyerhaus read the material which came out of the World Council meeting at Uppsala, he was galvanized into action. This led to the writing of this book as well as the publication of the Frankfurt Declaration.

During the summer of 1970 I visited with Professor Beyerhaus at Tübingen, at which time I asked him certain questions. One of the questions was this: "What do the German professors think about your work?" He replied that many of the professors in Germany who are non-evangelical were hostile to his work and were completely in disagreement with what he had done. He further indicated that the ecumenical movement was quite unhappy with the Frankfurt Declaration which sprang out of his book on humanization. I asked Professor Beyerhaus if he realized what his criticism of the ecumenical movement might lead to and whether he was willing to bear the opprobrium that was sure to come as a result of what he had written. Beyerhaus assured me that he had weighed the consequences carefully but that conscience demanded that he be faithful to the biblical revelation in the Scriptures. He was convinced that the World Council of Churches was moving in the wrong direction and that someone had to challenge its present stance. He felt that perhaps the time would shortly come when European evangelicals might be forced to dissociate themselves from the ecumenical movement to guarantee the purity of the message of the Gospel.

What Professor Beyerhaus has said needs to be read by every evangelical in America who seeks to understand and interpret the German and the European scene. It is clear that he writes from a German and from a Lutheran perspective. As one who does not stand in the Lutheran tradition I am not in full agreement with some of the things which he writes, but on the whole, his main thesis is quite tenable. If the book has a major fault it lies at the level of Professor Beyerhaus's interpretation and understanding of the contemporary evangelical scene in the United States of America. One cannot expect him to understand fully the situation in the United States any more than the average evangelical in the United States can fully comprehend the tides that flow in Germany and in Europe. But I do not think that what he says about evangelicals in the United States should cause anyone to overlook his major message which has to do with Europe and with the ecumenical movement as represented by the World Council of Churches. In a sense not clearly perceived by Professor Beyerhaus, many evangelicals in America have already crossed their Rubicon and have paid the price for opposing the policies of ecclesiastical bureaucrats in liberalized and secularized denominations who have turned from the evangelism of the New Testament to a view of the mission of the Church that seeks to change the social and the political structures.

It is yet too early to predict what the ultimate consequences of this movement by Beyerhaus and some of his missionary colleagues in Germany will be. But the very fact that the thesis articulated in this book has emerged from German scholarship is a marked departure from traditional happenings in that country in the twentieth century.

I strongly recommend that evangelicals everywhere who are interested in New Testament evangelism designed to reach every person with the Gospel of Jesus Christ read this very helpful work.

HAROLD LINDSELL
Editor, *Christianity Today*

Introduction

The word "mission" today has become an ambiguous concept. In both church and general usage, it has undergone a serious *de-valuation* and a serious *re-valuation*. The devaluation has occurred because traditional missionary activity, particularly in western churches and societies, has been hopelessly bound up with a terminated and isolated phase of history ("the Vasco-da-Gama-Epoch") from which it can no longer extricate itself. The revaluation has occurred because, in describing the totality of both the Church's and the world's basic desire for commitment in a particular situation, world mission today is understood in a variety of ways. Ernst Käsemann's statement, "In the future, there will be only one form of Christianity — mission" [1] is characteristic of this broader understanding. It is precisely this broader and increasingly more popular understanding which makes agreement on a clear definition of mission virtually impossible today for those of us involved in missiology.

Because of the wide range of opinions regarding the Church's missionary task and the practical application of this task, a strong tension has developed within the international missionary movement itself. Today two

[1] E. Käsemann, "Die Gegenwart des Gekreuzigten," *Christus unter uns*: Vorträge in der Arbeitsgruppe Bibel und Gemeinde des 13. Deutschen Evangelischen Kirchentags Hannover 1967, Stuttgart- Berlin (1967) p. 16.

contradictory points of view, the "evangelical" and the "ecumenical," stand over against each other. [2]

Certainly this contradiction appears radically in some organizations, but it is not confined to certain groups. It does, in fact, pervade practically all churches, councils, and missionary societies. This is the main reason why — in spite of the breakthrough in theological insight concerning the real unity of Church and mission — the great missionary awakening of the churches (which was expected from the 1961 merger of the International Missionary Council and the World Council of Churches) has not yet occurred. The same is true within the German setting.

[2] In this study, when the term "ecumenical" appears in quotation marks it is used in the narrow sense of the word as opposed to the broader concept of *ecumenical* or *oikumene*. In its narrower meaning it does not merely characterize the theology or an official position of the World Council of Churches and its organizations, but it refers to a current trend within those churches which are members of the World Council of Churches and among some of that organization's influential theologians. This trend has been the impetus for a critique of those "conservative evangelicals" outside the *oikumene*. In this specific sense, the term "ecumenical-evangelical" or "ecumenical-conservative" has to some extent already been recognized officially and often appears in current ecumenical discussions. Even though we formulate a criticism of the so-called "ecumenical" attitude, this is not meant to imply a basic reservation over against the ecumenical movement as a movement toward true Christian unity.

THE CRISIS IN THE CLASSICAL
UNDERSTANDING OF MISSION

Chapter I

THE CRISIS IN THE CLASSICAL
UNDERSTANDING OF MISSION

To analyze the present crisis in world missions with regard to its motivation and its goal, we must first consider how mission traditionally understands itself. There have been basic interests expressed in all of the various denominations and in the various changes in motives.

In spite of confessional differences, occasional distortions, and different emphases, these basic interests still allow the mission of our fathers to appear as a unified whole. In foreign missions, their interest was to proclaim the Gospel of Jesus Christ as the one divine Lord and Savior to the people of other lands. Non-Christians are to be converted, new churches established, and, above all, the name and the plan of salvation of the triune God are to be glorified.

As early as the seventeenth century, the Dutch theologian Voetius in his *Politica Ecclesiastica* expressed the task of mission as being three-fold: 1) to convert the heathen, 2) to establish churches, and 3) to glorify and proclaim divine grace. Walter Freytag concluded, "In mission, the Church understands herself to be that activity of God which takes place between the resurrection and the second coming. Through this activity under the message of the lordship of Him who died and was raised on our behalf, men are called to repentance; through baptism, they are gathered unto His people." [1]

This comprehensive goal was both a *universal* and an *urgent* one. The lordship of Christ was recognized as being valid for all peoples, and that salvation which He earned was, without exception, intended for every man. For this reason, inherent in mission is a vital holy impatience, an insatiable reaching out into all those areas which have not yet been penetrated by the Gospel; in other words, the Gospel must go to the farthest ends of the earth. The first General Assembly of the World Council of Churches in Amsterdam (1948) could then still say, "If the Gospel really is a matter of life and death, it seems intolerable that any human being now in the world should live out his life without ever having the chance to hear and receive it." [2]

How then in recent years could such a fundamental crisis develop within this movement which up to now had been so united and dynamic? Four basic reasons can be given:

1) In spite of its worldwide dimension and goal,

[1] W. Freytag, "Zwischenkirchlichen Hilfe und Internationaler Missionsrat," *Reden und Aufsätze*, Part II, Munich (1961) p. 85.

[2] *The First Assembly of the World Council of Churches*, W. A. Visser 'tHooft, ed., London, SCM (1969) p. 70. *Drafts for Sections prepared for the Fourth Assembly of the World Council of Churches, Uppsala, Sweden, 1968*, Geneva, (1968).

mission has been essentially centered in the western churches and carried on by western missions. In the period following World War II, the liberation of the Afro-Asian nations from colonial supremacy also brought about the independence of the younger churches. In spite of lengthy negotiations regarding the new partnership between older and younger churches for the continuation of mission, the concept of "mission" for many of the younger churches was emotionally saddled with the unpleasant memory of their former second-rate status.

2) In part, the Afro-Asian Christians were swept up in the nationalistic anti-western reaction of their non-Christian fellow countrymen. At the same time, however, this nationalistic reaction brought about a renaissance of the old religions. In its tendency to equate native nationality with adherence to ancestral religion, mission was understood as a disguised attempt to prolong the West's spiritual domination of Asia. Mission, understood as the winning of members from one religion to another, was accordingly branded as "proselytism." An attempt was made to curtail such activity by restrictive legislation. In India particularly, this conflict has affected the native Christians, both among the laity and the church officials, as well as the influential men involved in the mission.

The result has been that people began to dissociate themselves from such "proselytism." At this point, however, there is also the danger of sacrificing, in principle at least, the decisive goals of true mission. The question concerning the extent to which the Church's proclamation of the Gospel is directed toward conversion, baptism, and the establishing of new congregations in non-

Christian surroundings, is being discussed heatedly in India today.

3) Certain recent developments in western theology lend themselves to the Asiatic inclination toward religious co-existence and syncretism. In America, for example, within the Tillichian school, there has been a revival of Ernst Troeltsch's idea that, in principle, all religions share a common ground of being and, therefore, are to be understood as various culturally and historically conditioned expressions and as developmental states of the religious experience of that same transcendent ground of being. [3]

According to this view, the aim of the encounter among members of various religions ought not be conversion but rather only a mutually enriching *dialogue* and a final understanding. Today in Catholic dogmatics, we also find a "theology of religions." Here other religions are understood as participating both in the revelation and in that grace which is given for the sake of Christ. According to Heinz Robert Schlette, these religions are the "ordinary ways of salvation" for their followers, while Christianity is the "extraordinary way of salvation." [4] The logical result is that Christian missions are de-sensitized in their confrontation-consciousness.

4) A final crucial undermining of the traditional understanding of mission is the recent, radical supplanting of all basic religious issues by political-social concerns. This movement permeates all cultural spheres today

[3] P. Tillich, *Christianity and the Encounter of the World Religions,* New York, Columbia University Press (1963) pp. 27-51. Also *Systematic Theology,* Vol. I, Chicago (1951) pp. 18-21.
[4] H. R. Schlette, *Towards a Theology of Religions,* London (1963).

and its influence has been felt even in the Christian churches, particularly among young people. Friedrich Gogarten, [5] Ahrend van Leeuwen, [6] Harvey Cox, [7] and M. M. Thomas [8] are connected with an influential theological trend which interprets and justifies the secularization process as being a legitimate fruit of the Gospel. Because of this trend, theological interest moves away from the vertical dimension to the horizontal, i.e., away from the religious relation between God and man to the social relation between man and society. History becomes the important theological category. This history is not that specific salvation-history qualified by grace in Christ, but rather a world history standing under the lordship of Christ.

In the course of this universal post-war movement, a radical shifting of interest took place within the World Student Christian Federation, which up until this time had presented the strongest personal potential for world mission. It was the shift from John Mott's once evangelistic enthusiasm to an even greater socio-ethical enthusiasm. Today's students do not regard this change as a betrayal of the old missionary interests but rather just the opposite — as the legitimate realiza-

[5] L. Shier, *The Secularization of History:* An Introduction to the Theology of Friedrich Gogarten, Nashville (1966).

[6] A. van Leeuwen, *Christianity in World History:* The Meeting of the Faiths of East and West, New York (1965).

[7] H. Cox, *The Secular City,* New York (1965) and *On Not Leaving It to the Snake,* New York (1964). H. Cox along with J. C. Hoekendijk are theological contributors to the North American Study Group on Questions of Proclamation and its report, "The Church for the World." (Cf. chapter 2, footnote 11.)

[8] In regard to M. M. Thomas, cf. *The Christian Response to the Asian Revolution,* London, SCM (1966). Cf. also "A Dialogue between H. Berkhof and M. M. Thomas," *Secular Man and Christian Mission,* P. Löffler, ed., Geneva (1968) pp. 14-23.

tion of these interests within the changed conditions of today's world. [9]

These intellectual leaders of the World Student Christian Federation have been influential in bringing this new understanding of mission to bear upon the World Council of Churches.

---

[9] "The Christian Community in the Academic World" (a statement approved by the General Committee of the World Student Christian Federation), Geneva, 1964, p. 4; reprinted in *Student World* (1965) pp. 233-35.

THREE ANSWERS TO THIS CRISIS

Chapter II

THREE ANSWERS TO THIS CRISIS

Up to now how has Protestant Christianity in its mission responded to these four radical challenges after World War II? Originally, we could pick out three types of answers to this crisis, but these three, in the meantime, have been reduced to two. These three answers are:

First, the "conservative evangelicals'" intensification of previous evangelistic missionary activity on the basis of the defiant "nevertheless" of faith.

Second, the International Missionary Council's endeavors to achieve both a purer and firmer theological foundation and a new ecumenical form of mission. After the merger of the International Missionary Council with the World Council of Churches, these endeavors led to the

Third answer, namely, a totally new understanding of mission by theological leaders throughout the world in accommodation to the contemporary movements just mentioned. This understanding became influential in the Department on Mission Studies and on Studies in Evangelism in Geneva. [1]

1) The first answer, the intensification of previous missionary activity on the basis of the "nevertheless" of faith, can be illustrated in many missionary societies which are included in the traditional type of "faith mission," particularly in North America. Because of the theological position of these societies, they are called *conservative-evangelical.*

Today, in sharp contrast to the earlier assumed or actual stagnation of universal missionary activity, we should realize that the number of foreign missionaries and the amount of money donated for missions since World War II has not declined but, in reality, has increased. This growth in potential power, however, is only partially available to those denominational missions which are members of conciliar organizations. Basically, we are concerned with a variety of free missionary organizations which were constituted on the basis of faith and alliance. Most of these organizations are critical of the ecumenically-oriented societies and church missions. Today they already represent approximately 55 percent of all Protestant missionaries in the world.

Many of these missions have a history going back to the late nineteenth century. They developed from the "Second Revival." Others, however, have been formed only recently. Over and above this, many

[1] The collection of essays, *Protestant Cross-currents in Mission: The Ecumenical-Conservative Encounter,* Norman A. Horner, ed., Nashville, Abingdon Press (1968), reflects the typical contrasting understanding of the theology of mission as represented by three (moderate) "ecumenicals" and conservative evangelicals.

ecumenically-organized missions are in sympathy with them. Theologically, they all have an extremely conservative orientation. They strongly emphasize personal salvation as the heart of the Christian faith. The main concern of the Gospel for them is the reconciliation between God and man by Jesus Christ's saving sacrifice on the cross. As they see it, the teaching concerning personal salvation is being threatened by the ecumenically-oriented churches and missions.

A strong evangelistic intensity characterizes these missions. Their concern is the proclamation of salvation in Jesus Christ to non-Christians, particularly those who have never before heard the Gospel. This concern cannot be compromised. They prefer, therefore, to operate pioneer-missions which, in their opinion, are the real and truest form of missions. At the same time, a weakness is certainly inherent in this uncompromising attitude. Their endeavors frequently by-pass the younger ⊬ churches which have developed from previous missionary labors. They direct their attention to newly-opened-up or, up to now, little-touched areas and to the new languages and dialects into which the Bible may be translated. The American missiologist Pierce Beaver has called this movement the "Second Missionary Movement." [2]

Certainly they understand themselves to be the legitimate heirs of that former great missionary movement which in the early twentieth century culminated in John Mott's Student Voluntary Movement. They have taken up the classical slogan: "The Evangelization of the World in This Generation."

[2] P. Beaver, *From Mission to Mission*, New York (1964) p. 100.

The conservative evangelicals' missions have had their own overlapping alliances in the "Interdenominational Foreign Missionary Association" (I.F.M.A.) and the "Evangelical Foreign Missionary Association" (E. F.M.A.). [3] In the 1966 convention held in Wheaton, Illinois, the delegates attempted to clarify their theological bases and missionary principles. Opposing the development (partially evaluated as distortions) of missionary thought in the *oikumene,* they formulated their official statement in the significant *Wheaton Declaration.* [4] This declaration concluded in a solemn and expressive statement of self-dedication by the delegates present:

"In the support of this declaration
we
    the delegates here assembled in adoration to the
    Triune God, with full confidence in Holy Scripture,
    in submission to the Lord Jesus Christ, and looking
    for His coming again,
do covenant together
    for God's eternal glory, and in response to the Holy
    Spirit, with renewed dedication and in our oneness
    in Christ as the people of God,
to seek

[3] See the following books by D. A. McGavran:
   The Bridges of God, London (1955);
   How Churches Grow, London (1959);
   Church Growth and Group Conversion, D. A. McGavran, ed.,
      Lucknow (1962[3]);
   Understanding Church Growth, Eerdmans (1970).
[4] Reprinted in *International Review of Missions* (IRM) (October, 1966) pp. 458-76. Cf. also the collection of official reports, *The Church's Worldwide Mission,* Harold Lindsell, ed., Word Books, Waco, Texas (1966).

under the leadership of our Head with full assur-
ance of His power and presence,
the mobilization of the Church
its people, its prayers and resources,
for the evangelization of the world in this generation,
so help us God!
Amen." [5]

2) In contrast to the revival of the traditional missionary goals by the conservative evangelicals, the
International Missionary Council saw a judgment of
God in the revolutionary events during and after the
war. This challenged them to examine carefully their
earlier missionary theories and methods. They regarded the fusion of true missionary obedience with
involvement in national or church-political interests,
the sharing in the typical western cultural superiority
of the colonial period, and the organizational separation
of the missionary activity of particular missionary societies from the Church's total spiritual commitment as being serious spiritual and structural drawbacks to true
mission. This condition was to be overcome by theological reflection on the biblical foundations of mission and
by corresponding ecumenical action. The International
Missionary Council's first two conferences after the war
in Whitby (1947) and Willingen (1952), as well as
the World Council of Churches' first two General Assemblies in Amsterdam (1948) and Evanston (1954),
stood particularly under the shadow of this theological
reconsideration of mission and its new ecumenical approach. Nevertheless, there was a basic continuity

5 IRM (October, 1966) pp. 475-76.

with the spiritual desires expressed by the pioneers of this ecumenical missionary movement, as they were clarified theologically at the three earlier World Missionary Conferences in Edinburgh, Jerusalem, and Tambaram. In part, what some of the most farsighted theologians such as Karl Heim, Hendrik Kraemer, Karl Hartenstein, Walter Freytag, and Max Warren had tried without success to assert both in 1928 and in 1938, now, because of the cleansing fire of World War II, found ready acceptance. The strict eschatological understanding of mission in particular is an example of this. Mission, from this point of view, basically means the gathering together under the cross of the Messianic salvation-community which looks toward that promised kingdom to be expected at the second coming of Christ.

The idea that mission and Church are closely related and that during the period between Christ's ascension and His second coming the Church is placed in the world for the sake of mission, was even more important for the leaders of the International Missionary Movement. Because of this purpose of the Church, mission is not the concern of some specialists or societies, but rather the concern of the whole Church. Kraemer, correspondingly, wrote his *Theology of Laity*. [6] By overstating certain of his points, his Dutch students developed their "Theology of the Apostolate." [7] In this "Theology of the Apostolate" the Church is

[6] H. Kraemer, *Theology of Laity*, London (1958).

[7] Cf. A. A. van Ruler, "Theologie des Apostolates,"; *Evangelische Missions Zeitschrift* (1954) pp. 1-21 (with extensive bibliography). E. Jansen-Schoonhoven, "Der Artikel 'Vom Apostolat der Kirche' in der Kirchenordnung der niederländisch-reformierten Kirche," *Basileia*: Festschrift — Walter Freytag, J. Hermelink, H. J. Margull, eds., Stuttgart (1959) pp. 278-84.

understood as a missionary institution. Its sending precedes its gathering. Here we find those theological jumping-off points which later were incorporated into and further developed in the World Council of Churches' new understanding of mission.

From an organizational point of view, this emphasis on the unity between mission and Church led to the merging of the International Missionary Council with the World Council of Churches. The historic decision to unite the central organs of both these ecumenical movements, the Church-*oikumene* and the mission-*oikumene,* was strongly contested, particularly by the missions. [8] The high hopes of the advocates of the merger stood in contrast to their opponents' apprehension. The advocates of the merger hoped for an intensification of the missionary movement because they would thereby be accepted by the official churches. On the other hand, opponents of the merger, particularly those tending toward the evangelical position, feared that mission would become inflexible and bureaucratic. Above all, they feared the likelihood of a change in its true spiritual goal. Which of the two groups was to prove correct?

To begin with, the hopes of the advocates of the merger appeared to be moving toward fufillment. In New Delhi, the previous International Missionary Council was incorporated into the World Council of Churches as a new Commission and Division of World Mission and Evangelism. According to its constitution, it was given the task of seeing that "the Gospel of Jesus Christ be proclaimed in the whole world so

[8] N. Karlström, *Ökumene in Mission und Kirche,* Munich (1962) pp. 233-66.

that all men might believe in Him and be saved."
Over and above this, however, it was to support the
readiness for evangelism and mission in the whole
life and work of the World Council of Churches.

During the seven years between the Third and the
Fourth General Assemblies, series of tasks were re-
sumed or initiated by the ecumenical Division of World
Mission and Evangelism which attempted to take these
goals into consideration. Philip Potter, the present
director of this Division, has recently compiled an
impressive catalogue in which eight new activities,
study projects, and initiatory ecumenical contacts are
represented as being in the missionary interest of the
entire Church. [9] The selection of the new slogan, "Mission in Six Continents," the Study on the Structure of
the Missionary Congregation, the World Studies on
Churches in Mission, the "Healing Ministry of the
Church" project, the World-wide Project of Urban
and Industrial Mission, aid to the younger churches
for theological education, and the formation of a World
Association for Christian Communication are mentioned. In conjunction with these studies and activities, there are discussions with the conservative evangelicals on Church growth and with the Roman
Catholics on the missionary activity of the Church.

This is certainly an impressive list with numerous
respectable achievements. There is no question that
the missionary outreach of the Church — even in regard to the goals of the earlier International Missionary
Council — has been furthered and will continue to be

---

[9] Philip Potter, "Towards Renewal in Mission," *The Church Crossing Frontiers:* Essays on the Nature of Mission in Honour of Bengt
Sundkler; P. Beyerhaus, C. F. Hallenkreutz, eds., Lund (1969) pp.
244-46.

furthered by this. If, however, one tries to analyze and evaluate the whole development which the integrated world mission has taken under its new ecumenical leadership, many of those who had warned against the merger will subsequently find in it a confirmation of their theological apprehension.

3) Thus I proceed to the third answer for the radical crisis in mission, namely, that of a completely new understanding of mission on the part of the influential leaders in the World Council of Churches. I am fully aware that, in the face of the multiplicity of theological trends and denominational traditions in the World Council, one cannot speak of a uniform theology acceptable to all parties — even in the theology of mission. Nevertheless, in the official study documents published by the Division, we see a particular theological base establishing itself with increasing strength. It is this base of theological thought which influenced the discussion and statements of the study project on the Structure of the Missionary Congregation. Philip Potter himself has characterized this as one of the most significant studies which has ever been undertaken by the World Council of Churches. Its results are found in the collection of essays, *Planning for Mission,* [10] and in the official final report, *The Church for Others.* [11]

The Geneva staff attempted to validate this theological line of thinking. This is illustrated above all in its control over the Draft for Section 2 of the Uppsala

[10] Thomas Wieser, ed., *Planning for Mission,* London (1966).

[11] *The Church for Others and the Church for the World:* A Quest for Structures for Missionary Congregations, World Council of Churches, Geneva (1967).

Assembly [12] which was formulated by Walter Hollenweger. This control became even more obvious when
the staff stubbornly defended the Draft in a way which
was unacceptable according to the ecumenical rules
of the game, for. there were strong objections raised
against it from many sides, both immediately after
its publication and at the beginning of the Uppsala
Assembly, and a number of alternative outlines had
been presented. [13] The delegates to the section, however, immediately rejected the Draft by an overwhelm-
ing majority. It was then quickly replaced by one
newly formulated by Dr. John V. Taylor. Even so,
the editorial committee of the second sub-section of
Section 2 managed to push through definite ideas and
formulations in the second part of this final report.
According to the evangelical delegates, the acceptance
of this report did not entirely represent the actual
votes of the delegates. Instead of allowing the representatives of its member churches to arrive at theological conclusions freely, the administrative powers ap-
plied pressure for the acceptance of a basic ideal which
they themselves had formulated in advance. Seldom
in the history of the World Council has such a tendency to force an issue been so obvious as here.

Where then do we find Geneva's new concept of
mission? How did this concept replace the traditional
mission-concept of the International Missionary Council so quickly?

The basic components of the new "ecumenical" view

[12] Drafts for Sections prepared for the Fourth Assembly of the
World Council of Churches, Geneva (1968) pp. 28-51.
[13] B. Sundkler, "Uppsala 68," *Svensk Missionstidskrift* (1968) pp.
135-37.

of mission are outlined as follows: [14] The theological understanding of mission does not proceed from Christ's Great Commission to His Church, but rather from the sovereign activity of God in the world. God has been continually active in the world from the very beginning and, as such, is a "missionary" God. Through a series of interventions and revolutionary acts, God leads the world toward its goal. This goal, the Kingdom of God, is determined by Him. This kingdom is understood as a future kingdom but also as a thoroughly worldly one. It is a state of perfect peace and of prosperity for mankind: "Steadfast love and faithfulness will meet; righteousness and peace will kiss each other . . . and our land will yield its increase" (Ps. 85:10-12, RSV). [15]

Salvation is finally revealed in world history itself — a history which is theologically glorified. J. C. Hoekendijk, [16] the *spiritus rector* behind this idea, characterizes salvation as *shalom* (peace) — in a conscious but certainly undifferentiated reference to the Old Testament expectation. (Note: the New Testament concept of peace *[eirene]* is deliberately avoided because *shalom* more adequately expresses the fuller, i.e., the this-world-oriented, view. *Eirene,* however, characterizes man's new relationship to God which is based

[14] A pregnant representation and critique of the study-group for the structure of the missionary congregation's theological presuppositions is presented by H. T. Neve, *Sources for Change:* Searching for Flexible Church Structures, Geneva (1968) pp. 51-100. Cf. also the appended discussion in *Concept:* Arbeiten aus dem Referat für Fragen der Verkündigung, Special Issues 15 (July, 1967) and 19 (November, 1968).

[15] J. C. Hoekendijk, "Notes on the Meaning of Mission(ary)," *Planning for Mission,* pp. 42f.

[16] J. C. Hoekendijk, *The Church Inside Out,* London, SCM (1967).

on a reconciliation in Christ. This reconciliation can
be received only by faith.) Salvation history is not
understood here in the same way as in the Synoptics
and Acts. That is to say, it is not understood as a
history of the proclamation of the Gospel in which
world affairs constitute the background. Rather, God's
intervention in world events turns world history into
salvation history by overcoming evil powers. In those
historical revolutions brought about by God, the good
continually approaches us through the *Missio Dei*
which is active here. *New* and *good* are correlatives
just as *old* and *evil* are. To be a Christian means,
then, to desire the new and to participate actively in
change. [17]

What function does the Church have in God's activity in the world? It is in no way an end in itself.
It can never be the starting point or even the goal
of mission. It is not the mediator of a salvation which
it already has. Rather, salvation, the *shalom,* occurs
in the world, and the Church herself has only that
amount of salvation which she presently shares with
the world. [18] The Church, then, is not understood in
terms of her essence but rather in terms of her function. Her task is to reach transformingly into worldly
events by participating in the *Missio Dei.* If she does
not do this, she becomes a useless instrument. However,
if the Church fails, God will achieve His goal without
her. [19] The Church is not closer to God than the world

[17] "Mission in God's Mission," *Planning for Mission*, p. 50.
[18] J. C. Hoekendijk, *Planning for Mission*, p. 44.
[19] "Only if we believe that our Father is making all things new,
will we dare to make our business the problems on the world's
agenda. Certainly renewal does not depend on our understanding

is. The idea of His sacramental presence in the Church is rejected because that is a heathen idea representing God as Baal, as a God-in-residence. [20]

The Church is a part of the world. The only difference between her and the rest of the world is that, because of her knowledge of the saving goal of history, the Church now marches ahead of the rest of humanity as the vanguard in the movement toward this goal. [21]

Here the idea of a *frontier* between Church and world, which serves as a line of demarcation between the saved and the unsaved, between belief and unbelief, is rejected. [22] Mission is then no longer a calling to men to cross the frontier. On the one hand, God has already reconciled the whole world to Himself in that salvation which was completed by Christ. On the other hand, both belief and unbelief are found in the heart of every single Christian. There are neither geographical frontiers which the Christian missionary must cross nor frontiers of faith which he must call others to cross. In an over-stated form, we see in this Karl Barth's theological influence, especially in regard to his doctrine of baptism.

or misunderstanding of what God is doing in His Son. All that is at stake is whether we are working with Him or against Him." *Drafts for Sections,* 29. Cf. also footnote 21.

[20] J. C. Hoekendijk, *Planning for Mission,* p. 42.

[21] "The World in the Setting of Historical Change and Eschatological Hope" (Western European Work-Group), *Planning for Mission,* p. 81. Cf. also the following quotation from P. Keller, "The World in Transformation," *Planning for Mission,* p. 72: "Christ is only seen to act in the world today by these links of Church or Bible, of Sacrament and faith, so that the institutions themselves become mediators, as guardians of the sacraments or the Book. The Church is not a segment of the world but a radically different element. Clericalism is the consequence and expression of this fact."

[22] J. C. Hoekendijk, *Planning for Mission,* p. 40.

What then is meant by *mission?* The concept of
mission acquires a completely new content. Mission is
the total responsibility of the Church for the world. [23]
Since the Church exists only in this responsibility for
the world as the "Church for others," she is either
mission in everything she does or she is nothing. For
this "pro-existence," she must radically change her
structures; she must re-transform herself from a "come-
structure," the gathered community drawn to the center of its worship, into a "go-structure," which is
oriented toward action in the world. [24] To specify
certain activities as mission — for example, the proclamation of the Gospel to non-Christians — would be
wholly arbitrary for this understanding. Hence, this
new concept could easily divert attention from the
Church's crucial tasks today to less relevant ones. Because mission is participation in the *Missio Dei,* it always occurs in those places in the world where God
is most dynamically active, according to Richard Shaull,
the theologian of revolution. [25] God is active in the
great revolutionary movements of our time, in the
fight for racial equality, and in the attempts for edu-
cational reform at the college and university level. In

[23] J. C. Hoekendijk, *Ibid.,* pp. 37f. "Contrary to a widespread
opinion, the recent reintroduction of the term *Apostolate* (apostolé)
to indicate *all aspects of the pro-existent nature and ministry of the
Church is not a 'modern innovation'.*" M. Linz similarly calls the
essence of mission, man's collaboration in the work of God within
the whole area of human historical life in this world. Cf. *Anwalt der
Welt,* Stuttgart-Berlin (1964) pp. 210-15.

[24] H. J. Margull, "Gemeinden für andere," *Mission als Struktur-
prinzip, Geneva* (1968 [3]) p. 7.

[25] R. Shaull, "The Revolutionary Challenge to Church and Theology," *Theology Today* XXIII (1967) p. 479. "It requires . . . a new
involvement in those places in the world where God is most dynamically at work."

principle, God is active in such efforts in all six continents; in Harlem as well as in Heidelberg and Hawaii.

Now we understand why only in the second of the
three sub-sections of Uppsala's Section 2 the Geneva
staff was so interested in pushing its idea through. The
special theme of this second sub-section was: "Opportunities for Mission." [26] The intention was to replace
the old idea of ethnic and religious mission fields,
which tend to be localized in the southern hemisphere,
with a new historical-theological understanding of the
special opportunities for missionary activity within
present political-social events. For this reason, the influential members of this group refused to take seriously a delegate who referred to the statement of the
conservative-evangelical, Prof. McGavran, that there
are two billion people who have not yet heard or have
not yet accepted the Gospel of Christ. [27]

Expecting this situation, McGavran had provokingly
formulated his argument in the lead-article in his
Church Growth Bulletin, "Will Uppsala Betray the
Two Billions?" [28] "Ecumenicals" and evangelicals in
the section were engaged in heated arguments as to

[26] *The Uppsala Report 1968*, N. Goodall, ed., Geneva (1968) p. 30.
[27] Communicated by Canon D. Webster, April 26, 1969, in Tübingen, Germany.
[28] *Church Growth Bulletin*, Vol. IV, No. 5 (May, 1968) p. 1. The
reference to the two billion not-yet-Christian people comes from the
mission decree *"Ad Gentes."* "The Church is aware that there still
remains a gigantic missionary task for her to accomplish. For the
Gospel message has not yet been heard, or scarcely so, by two
billion human beings. And their number is increasing daily. They
are formed into large and distinct groups by permanent cultural ties,
by ancient religious traditions, and by firm bond of social necessity."
"Decree on the Missionary Activity of Church," *The Documents of
Vatican II*, Walter M. Abbott, S. J., ed., Guild Press, New York,
p. 597.

whether this reference should be accepted or not. Although there were strong objections on the part of
some, the sentence, "The church has an irrevocable
responsibility for the hundreds of millions" — the two
billion, in the meantime had shrunk — ". . . to acquaint
those who have not yet heard the Gospel of God's forgiveness in Christ with this Gospel," was tacked onto
the final report. In the official English version of the
Uppsala Report it first appeared in the third revised
edition. The sentence is certainly prominent in its
present context, but, since the whole Uppsala Section 2
report, in general, is a conglomerate of contradictory
concepts of mission, that statement has no relationship
to the whole. [29] While this document reflects a variety
of opinions, it does not present a comprehensive theological view of Church and mission. [30]

[29] J. R. W. Stott calls the reference " . . . still very inadequate and
largely swallowed up in a mass of other material." "Why I was disturbed," *Church of England Newspaper* (August 23, 1968).

[30] Cf. U. Fick's criticism "Missions als Auskunft über das Motive
meines Handeln?" *Oekumenische Rundschau* (1969) particularly pp.
39-42.

THE "ECUMENICAL-EVANGELICAL" CONFRONTATION

Chapter III

THE "ECUMENICAL-EVANGELICAL" CONFRONTATION

This brings us to the question of the ecumenical *consequences* of the present confrontation between the two understandings of mission — that of classical evangelism and that of an evolutionary theology of history. Up to now both understandings could be compared only as ideas but not according to power and organization. A large number of missionary organizations and missionaries fully support the evangelical view. The "ecumenical" understanding, on the other hand, is held by a few radical-minded representatives in the administration of the *oikumene* and its local organizations, in some experimental projects on the missionary front, and, finally, in theological teaching positions, particularly in Latin America. [1] The majority of missionary organizations

[1] Cf. C. Peter Wagner, *Latin American Theology: Radical or Evangelical?* Eerdmans (1970).

represented in the World Council of Churches, their missionaries, and their supporting congregations or individuals either support the theology of the former International Missionary Council or understand their position as being that of mere agents of inter-church aid. In spite of this, the so-called "ecumenical view" exerts an increasingly strong influence in missionary societies and the younger churches. Three reasons for this are:

First, their representatives, as we have seen, essentially control the study program of the ecumenically organized missions.

Second, in the pursuit of those biblical-theological statements made by the International Missionary Council, evangelistic-minded member missions of the World Council of Churches have up to now not been able to develop a concept with a similarly dynamic effect which could prove to be a *via media* between the two extremes. Walter Freytag and Karl Hartenstein are virtually ineffective. The evangelistic-oriented missions in the World Council up to now have not been able to recover from their post-war crisis. Therefore, their merger with the World Council has, in fact, changed nothing.

Third, (and this is the crucial reason), this briefly outlined, new ecumenical understanding of mission corresponds basically to that central theological idea which inspires the Church's avant-garde youth in the world today. At the same time, it corresponds in general to the basic theme of the World Council of Churches in its other divisions and commissions, and, last but not least, it is supported theoretically as well as practically by the members of the World Student Christian Federation.

The most agitating question for the Church today is the political-social question about world-wide justice and peace in our time, especially in view of the dynamic expectation of the Third World (that is, those nations of the world unaligned with either East or West). For this reason, the recent meetings which are considered to be most important in the *oikumene* itself are the Geneva Conference for Church and Society (1966) [2] and the Ecumenical-Catholic Conference for World-wide Cooperation in Questions of Development which was held in Beirut (April, 1968). [3] The whole Fourth World Council of Churches Assembly in Uppsala was influenced by these conferences and their line of reasoning.

This development is being met with loud protest from all those who today are committed to the original goals of the evangelistic missionary movement. This is true also of those conservative evangelistic missions outside the *oikumene*. Because of the events in Uppsala, these conservative evangelicals are now even more critical of ecumenical attempts to persuade them to join the World Council of Churches. What is more, those evangelicals who see their witness as a corrective from within the ecumenically integrated mission are becoming increasingly uneasy today.

The evangelicals' criticism of the working method and the section 2 report is forceful. [4] Canon Douglas Web-

[2] *World Conference on Church and Society:* Official Report World Council of Churches, Geneva (1967).

[3] *The Conference on World Cooperation for Development, Beirut, Lebanon, April 21-27, 1968:* Official Report World Council of Churches, Geneva (1968).

[4] *Church Growth Bulletin* (November, 1968) Uppsala Issue Number Three, A. Glasser, "What has been the Evangelical Stance, New Delhi to Uppsala?" *Evangelical Missions Quarterly* (Spring, 1969)

ster, in his sermon, "Bible and Mission," said scathingly, "I would hazard a guess that the time will come — perhaps soon — when those with the most knowledge and experience of real mission will consider the Uppsala report on mission to be little short of a sell-out to the diseased and confused spirit of our age. Its weakness is less in what it said than in what it refused to say." The criticism is made that this section was not able to arrive at a clear definition of its understanding of mission. The interest in the horizontal (i.e. social) dimension was so overpowering that the vertical dimension (i.e., the God-to-man relationship) simply did not receive the proper attention. An active minority of the delegates stubbornly withstood all attempts to acknowledge the basic evangelical priorities, namely, zeal for God's honor, the growth of the Church, personal decision, man's forsaken condition outside of Christ, and the central function of the proclamation of the Gospel. The evangelicals were regarded simply as "traditionalists" [5] by those convinced of the social-ethical ideal of mission. The evangelicals' point of view was not considered.

As a result, the evangelicals say that the great mis-

pp. 129-50. Critical voices of Norwegian pietism — the response was not uniform — are found in O. G. Myklebust's collection of newspaper articles, "etterslet fra Uppsala," *Norsk tidskrift for misjon*, No. 1 (1969) particularly pp. 44-46, 52-57.

[5] M. M. Thomas states that the traditionalists in Section 2, who were occupied with the theory of mission, were apparently very articulate. "Uppsala 1968 und die gegenwärtige theologische Lage," *Oekumenische Rundschau* (1969) p. 380. The youthful delegates and unofficial guests judged the assembly even more strongly: "One found oneself neatly labelled, and then consigned to one or other of two pigeonholes. Everybody was either a 'conservative,' 'traditionalist,' 'reactionary,' or 'status quo' person, or a radical revolutionary. . . ." J. R. W. Stott, *Church of England Newspaper* (August 23, 1968).

sionary possibilities for proclamation are silenced. Prof. McGavran, in retrospect, answers the provocative question which he threw out to the Assembly before its convocation, with a definitive "yes": "Uppsala betrayed the biblical concept of mission. . . ." [6] With the attempt to correct horizontal relationships, the spiritually starved masses have been led to place material values before spiritual. McGavran asks his evangelical friends to reject the Uppsala document as a guideline for future mission. Instead, they should energetically advance *that* program for mission and evangelism which God, in the past, has blessed. In this way, they would give a proper balance to service and proclamation in such a way that a maximum of new discipleship could develop. [7]

Today the American and many Norwegian evangelicals publicly characterize the New Delhi decision to merge the International Missionary Council with the World Council of Churches as a failure. [8] Uppsala itself has illustrated the wide-spread resignation which exists in regard to the work of evangelism and world mission. On the other hand, it is interesting to note that a professor of missiology at Dallas Theological Seminary has called this same period (1961-68) a new era of missionary proclamation. The evangelical wing of the Church of Jesus Christ has taken hold in this new era. Its new missionary *élan* sees undreamed-of possibilities in Latin America, Africa, and Asia. The consequences of the growing divergence could be extremely

[6] D. McGavran, *Church Growth Bulletin* (November, 1968) p. 44.
[7] *Ibid.*, p. 45.
[8] A. Glasser (cf. footnote 4) p. 131. Anonymous lead article in the Norwegian journal *Utsyn* (No. 16, 1968) written in regard to the official statements of the conference of evangelical Nordic student organizations, calls for the Norwegian state-church's withdrawal from the World Council of Churches and its organizations.

serious. The evangelicals, with increasing impatience, challenge the Geneva department of missions to consider their wishes by revising the present understanding of mission. Forces in the ecumenical camp, which are equally strong, oppose this and turn their backs on the evangelicals. There is the danger which Lesslie Newbigin prophesied as early as 1958, [9] namely, that the evangelicals might entirely renounce the World Council of Churches and revive the former International Missionary Council.

The Commission on World Mission and Evangelism is aware of this conflict. For this reason, its 1972 world mission conference (to be held in Indonesia) will deal with this set of questions. The planned topic is "Salvation Today!" The most difficult theological task which will have to be undertaken there is the counter-balancing of the evangelicals' desires with those of the ecumenical social ethicists.

It has become important for leading representatives in the World Council of Churches to listen to the conservative evangelicals in the future and to initiate constructive cooperation with the great group in Protestantism which up to now has been on the outside. Dr. Franklin Clark Fry, for many years the chairman of the Central Committee, explained in his posthumously published report that in the six years between the Third and the Fourth Assemblies the committee had assiduously striven without much success for closer contacts "with the deeply-committed and fervently Christian brethren at the other end of the spectrum." "We believe," Fry wrote, "that their entrance into the ecumen-

[9] L. Newbigin, *One Body, One Gospel, One World*, London, International Missionary Council (1958).

ical dialogue will lead to great mutual enrichment." [10]
The Assembly then resolved to ask the conservative
evangelicals to seek ways in which their "theological
convictions, spiritual experience, and missionary zeal
might well find some vital expression in the life of the
World Council of Churches." [11] This generous invita-
tion sounded quite hopeful. One will, however, have to
consider the evangelical reply given by Douglas Webster: "The right hand of fellowship which Uppsala held
out to these evangelicals will not be grasped while its
left hand holds the Bible so lightly." [12]

[10] *The Uppsala Report 1968*, p. 280.
[11] *Ibid.*, p. 185.
[12] Canon D. Webster, "Bible and Mission," Annual Sermon before the British and Foreign Bible Society, March 9, 1970, published
by the British and Foreign Bible Society, 1970, p. 8.

THE NECESSITY OF A
RECIPROCAL CORRECTIVE

Chapter IV

THE NECESSITY OF A
RECIPROCAL CORRECTIVE

In spite of everything, can we hope for a successful and theologically acceptable merger of the new "ecumenical" and "evangelical" views of mission in reciprocal correction and complement? Obviously both parties must be ready to have their positions, in their one-sidedness or even distortion, fundamentally called into question. What should this reciprocal corrective look like?

The legitimate objections which the *evangelicals* must face are as follows:

Without a doubt the strength of the evangelicals' position is that they understand the essence of mission in the light of unimpeachable biblical revelation: the statements which the Bible makes in regard to the basic situation of fallen mankind and God's eternal plan of salvation in the sending of His Son. But in their dog-

matic observation, as Martin L. Kretzmann [1] correctly
points out, their thinking is in danger of mistakenly as-
sociating itself with a closed theological system. In
this system the world is interpreted on the basis of a
static understanding of its relationship to ultimate
meaning and fulfillment. Thus, one does not really consider world history in its openness — which began with
the coming of Christ — and in the new unique challenges, offerings, and possibilities contained in it. Instead, the world is seen to be incurably evil and is
understood to be moving toward its destruction. Its
history has no positive meaning. The task of mission
is to save as many people as possible from this evil
world by proclaiming the immutable message of judgment and grace. Its task is also to bring men together
in rapidly growing churches. These churches are understood as lasting places of refuge or islands in the cata-
ract of time.

In the face of this radical, ontological, and eternity-
oriented thinking, the multiplicity of human cultures,
conditioned by creation and history, becomes less important. In the face of the radical dualistic view of
eternal blessing and eternal damnation, temporal or
social suffering and happiness easily become insignifi-
cant. In the light of the ultimate goal, this point of
view is certainly appropriately oriented. It can refer
to a great and vital tradition which goes all the way
back to the New Testament. Its weakness, however,
is its failure to understand the significance of the first
article of faith and, often, to relate itself to social prob-

[1] M. L. Kretzmann, "Salvation Today — Theological Issues," mimeographed paper, Division for World Mission and Evangelism, DWME
69/63, p. 1.

lems. The meaning inherent in a creation which was intended by God and is loved by Him, is overlooked by a dualism of salvation which at times appears practically Manichean.[2] This dualism also fails to recognize that this creation is not wholly negated through the incarnation and the new creation (which is the eschatological transformation of the original creation) but that it is overcome (in the dialectic sense of the word) by the love of God.

World history, then, is understood neither in its movement toward the *eschaton* under the lordship of the triune God, nor in its permanent inter-relationship to salvation history as both the external condition and the arena of salvation history. In this system's orientation toward ultimate realities, the fact that the eternal can also confront us in the temporal, i.e., the here and now, is overlooked — even when, in a state of constant change, it takes on a tangible form. It should then be obvious to the evangelicals as well that our eternal destiny will be determined in the Last Judgment on the basis of how we react to that Christ who anonymously confronts us in the midst of the historical conditions of a disordered society. Not only the souls but also the righteous deeds of the saints will enter into the coming glory.[3]

This particular rigidity of the evangelicals' point of view has further dangerous consequences. The evangelicals illegitimately absolutize their own ecclesiastical form by deluding themselves into thinking that they are the true representation of the ideal "invisible" Church

[2] The word is derived from Mani (A.D. 216-274) who supported a radical dualism between good and evil, light and darkness.
[3] Rev. 14:13.

or the congregation of Jesus. This attitude is the cause
of renewed divisions in Protestantism. Every new discovery of a cleavage between the ethical-dogmatic
ideal and the empirical form could cause a new separation and a withdrawal. In this separation, one is not
critical enough of the sinfulness of his own existence.
In missionary practice, this type of idealistic thinking
leads to a type of lasting paternalism, i.e., a hesitation
to give responsibility to the younger churches.

Another problem is the solidification in biblicalism
and fundamentalism of the evangelicals' perception of
truth. The legitimate emphasis on the Holy Bible as
the invariable norm and the only source of Christian
theology and proclamation can sometimes mean in
practice that the abundance of inexhaustible biblical
statements and one's own limited understanding of
Scripture are naively equated.

The rejection of the missionary dialogue as a means
of achieving a more profound knowledge of truth on
the part of the Christian participants in this dialogue
stems partially from the fact that the evangelical does
not want to recognize that God can lead us to a further
understanding of His Word by means of the questions
of the non-Christian who is also searching for truth.

The worst consequence of this extreme eschatological orientation is the exclusion of the biblical understanding of salvation from history and society. According to the evangelical understanding, salvation as a
corporate, visible event is a purely other-worldly treas-
ure of Christian hope. In this present age, it can only
be anticipated in the Christian's personal relationship
to Christ through faith and in the spiritual community
of the saved ones. It is not recognized that salvation

in a real way breaks into social conditions in history, and that it can and will transform man's relationship to his fellowman through forgiveness, love, and humility. Social structures are not simply unchangeable orders of creation and preservation. They are also a corporate expression of unique interpersonal relations which are perverted by egoism, the desire for power, and mistrust. For that reason, these structures must first be given over to the lordship of Christ.

The proclamation of salvation in Christ cannot be limited to a restoration of the vertical relationship between God and man, as the evangelicals too quickly try to do. This proclamation must also point out the beneficial as well as the obligatory consequences which arise from salvation for man's communal life, his families, tribes, classes, and races. It is true, the "merciful brother" can never replace the merciful God. However, the Christian who is socially insensitive should be made to realize his deficiency by pointing out to him the obvious social conflicts in which he as a man is involved. Although the vertical and the horizontal dimensions must be theologically and spiritually differentiated, they are not to be separated from each other in human life.

He who has recognized the theological relevance of horizontal relationships must also recognize that these relationships are constantly changing. This change is first really aroused by the Christian message. Therefore, the revolutionary tensions of our time confront us with the challenge of God as the Lord of history to make our proclamation in a non-Christian world understandably concrete. The world's agenda can neither place a limitation on the choice of topics for missionary

proclamation nor determine its contents. Rather, this
agenda raises important questions which deeply concern the members of human society, and to ignore
these problems in proclamation would be inexcusably
irresponsible. Although it is true that solidarity with
those who identify themselves with the humanization
of human life is no substitute for proclaiming the message of the crucified and risen Son of God, such solidarity is the indispensable pre-supposition and consequence of this proclamation today.

The present evangelical protest against ecumenical
"horizontalism," because of its one-sidedness, is most
certainly justified. But the answer to socio-ethical questions is not found by stubbornly ignoring them. This
would result in a self-imposed isolationism which, to
be sure, could not delay the great historical changes
of our time, but which, by our lack of involvement,
would expose us, when these changes prove to be cata-
strophic to humanity, to the judgment of God, the
Lord of Mission.

Still, it is possible that evangelical mission will open
itself up to that socio-ethical movement which permeates the whole of Christianity today. The relationship between evangelistic and diaconal purposes corresponds to the best traditions of evangelical piety. [4]
Evangelical Christianity can look back to noteworthy
achievements, particularly in the nineteenth century,
such as the successful battle against slavery and the
founding of the Red Cross. The hesitation of evangelicals in past decades to be involved in social service
ought to be understood as a reaction to that contem-

[4] Timothy Smith, *Revivalism and Social Reform in Mid-Nineteenth
Century America*, New York (1957).

porary tendency of the Church in which the call to a "social gospel" went hand in hand with a dangerously liberal undermining of the Christian message. Presently this tendency is even more pronounced and causes an even greater fear of producing a gospel of man's relationship to his fellowman which is simply oriented to this world.

In spite of this, however, the evangelicals turned with renewed interest to social issues in their "Wheaton Declaration." Holding firmly to the priority of proclamation, they committed themselves to invite the whole of evangelical Christianity to work "openly and firmly for racial equality, human freedom, and all forms of social justice throughout the world." [5] Even in Uppsala, the conservative evangelicals were heavily influenced by the dynamic of the challenge presented by the social problems of the Third World. In contrast to the earlier tendency of identifying mission with proclamation, Rev. John R. W. Stott, the main speaker for the evangelicals in Section 2, suggested this definition: "Mission equals proclamation plus service." [6]

Thus the problem of the relationship between proclamation and social activity, eternal salvation and improvement of living conditions in history, is resolved in practice but not in theology. In placing proclama-

[5] *International Review of Missions*, p. 474.
[6] J. R. W. Stott, "Does Section Two Provide Sufficient Emphasis on World Evangelism?" *Church Growth Bulletin* (Nov., 1968) p. 39. Cf. also A. R. Tippett's "The Call of God — to Proclaim and to Serve," *Cross-currents in Mission*: the Ecumenical-Conservative Encounter, Norman A. Horner, ed., Nashville (1968) pp. 64-78. Further, cf. D. McGavran, "Social Justice and Evangelism," *World Vision Magazine* (June, 1965). Cf. also the debate between G. Linnenbrink, H. Lindsell, and G. W. Webber concerning the topic, "Witness and Service," IRM (1965) pp. 428ff., 437ff., 441ff.

tion and service together, one can refer to the example of Jesus and the message of the prophets. However, there is still something of an undynamic and un-unified relationship between them. Only a profound understanding of the eschatological significance of world history can help the evangelicals out of their uncertainty.

The American Congress for Evangelism which took place in Minneapolis in September, 1969, was an important step in this direction. There were 4,600 participants from 100 denominations, inclusive of the Southern Baptists and the Missouri Synod Lutherans, who met together to discuss reports on the relationship between evangelism and social responsibility — particularly in terms of the race problem. A lead article in *Christianity Today* summarizes the situation as follows:

> The congress was willing to look deeply into the implications of the Gospel for the social *milieu*. Perhaps no evangelical conclave in this century has responded more positively to the call for Christians to help right wrongs in the social order.

It is important to note that the participants thus became aware of their own particular understanding of the steps which need to be taken:

> Those who listened carefully realized that the call to social involvement was put on a personal basis. Thus there was avoided what so many evangelicals believe to be a major error of the ecumenical movement, that of making the institutional church the agent of social revolution as though this were the mission of the Church. Believers, as members of Caesar's kingdom as well as of God's, were called upon to exercise their dual citizenship in such a way that their Christian faith would be

brought to bear upon society for constructive change. [7]

The critical objections to be raised in regard to the "Ecumenicals'" new understanding of mission are diametrically opposed to the above statements which were directed to the evangelicals' understanding of mission. Here world history is most certainly taken seriously as a central theological issue. World history, however, is seen in only one dimension. This one-sidedness involves a disastrous omission in view of the fact that the world will be called into account by eschatological judgment and in view of the promised apocalyptic new creation.

If the evangelical attempt consists of isolating unique salvation history from the total framework of world history in a gnostic way [8] (that is to say, as the history of a Church which has been freed from the world), then, for the "ecumenicals," salvation history is in danger of being subsumed under evolutionary world history.

To the "ecumenicals," history itself reveals the standard for missionary activity. Certainly the Bible and God's Self-revelation in Christ are still called upon. The Bible, however, serves more as an explication of empirical processes and, by doing so, no longer really transcends these processes. Missionary proclamation no longer has to bring that mysterious "new" which is totally different in its content, and which has promise of post-historical fulfillment. [9] Rather, it gives man the answers to those most profound existential questions

[7] *Christianity Today* (October 10, 1969) p. 32.

[8] Similar to the gnostic heresy of the Early Church era which understood salvation as the return of the soul from the evil "worldly" creation to the heavenly "world of Light."

[9] 1 Cor. 2:6-10.

which he confronts through his involvement in the historical process of revolution. There is no certainty that the missionary himself already understands the concrete forms of this answer. Instead, he must search for these forms through solidary self-involvement in the concrete situation and through dialogue with non-Christians. [10]

This new ecumenical understanding of dialogue carries with it a potential danger. Certainly a direct and convincing dialogue is a missionary method fully grounded in the New Testament. But in "ecumenical" literature this dialogue becomes a new source of revelation for the witness himself. This was obvious when in Uppsala a member of the Geneva administration tried to slip the following sentence into the section plan: "Christ speaks to us through the brother (i.e., the non-Christian) and, thereby, corrects our limited and distorted understanding of the witness." One of the delegates objected to this. If this sentence were accepted, he noted, the only reference in the whole paragraph to Christ's message would be His speaking through the non-Christian. Here the dialogue itself proclaims the Gospel to Christians by means of non-Christians! [11]

The ecumenical anticipation of *shalom* is basically directed toward a new inter-personal happening which places horizontal relationships on a more human level. [12]

[10] "In encounter with Moslems and Hindus, Marxists and humanists, Christians are learning to look for the basis of a common understanding of man, which will lead to a fuller apprehension of truth." *Draft for Sections*, p. 30.

[11] J. R. W. Stott, *Church of England Newspaper* (August 23, 1968).

[12] "Shalom is a *social happening*, an event in inter-human relations, a venture of co-humanity. . . ," J. C. Hoekendijk, "Notes on the Meaning of Mission(ary)," *Planning for Mission*, p. 43.

A confirmation of the age-old human desire to unite all of humanity in a truly human life is involved. This occurs, in intention at least, by referring to Jesus as the Beginner of a new humanity. [13] All men are called to participate in this new humanity. What is more, they have already been reborn as those who, in principle, are reconciled together. [14]

Note how, in the "ecumenicals'" view, the theological distinction between the *foundation* and the *appropriation* of salvation as expressed in 2 Corinthians 5:18-20 is blurred in a kind of universalism. In view of the reconciliation which was established by God through the cross of Christ for the whole of humanity, they fail to recognize that the individual man still lives in an unsaved condition until he is confronted with the event of the cross in the act of proclamation. Man is, in that proclamation, called upon to decide whether, in faith, he wants to accept or reject the offer of reconciliation. In the "ecumenicals'" universalism, however, it seems as if all of humanity since Golgotha is out of danger in regard to the coming judgment (that is, insofar as the New Testament teaching on judgment is still adhered to). [15] The social concern diverts one's attention from the metaphysical hunger, the eschatological threat.

Behind the social pathos of the "ecumenicals" there

[13] "Renewal in Mission," *Drafts for Sections, Uppsala 68*, p. 28.
[14] "By the raising up of the New Man, Christ Jesus, every man has been made a member of the new mankind," *Planning for Mission*, p. 54.
[15] Cf. W. Krusche's critique on the optimism of the theology of history regarding the studies on the structure of missionary congregations: "The emphasis in the ecumenical study on the prophetic task . . . does nevertheless have unmistakably enthusiastic traits." Herbert T. Neve, *Sources for Change*, World Council of Churches, Geneva (1968) pp. 90f.

is most certainly a real solidarity with the legitimate demands and expectations of that two-thirds of the world on the other side of the privileged Euro-American hemisphere which is threatened by unimaginable famine. We are also reminded of that denunciatory passion of the Old Testament prophets which was directed against the cults. The prophets called for a removal of that worship which was isolated from responsibility for one's fellowman. [16] However, might not such a legitimate criticism of a cultic pietism which is unconcerned about social ethics suddenly lead men to overlook man's unalterable *need for God,* especially because the social needs of the two billion non-Christians are so great? How important it is for the "ecumenical" whether man in the course of his life does or does not come into contact with the biblical God through the message of Christ?

Certainly, the "ecumenicals" can object that the Church's oral message loses its force of conviction in a non-Christian world when Christianity — which is predominantly Western — obviously ignores the social consequences of its faith. This criticism, however, is only partially valid. Happily, the path of the Gospel through the world is not bound to ethical, exemplary deeds of Western Christianity. Rather, the Afro-Asian and Latin-American Church stands on the brink of missionary possibilities which have seldom been seen in its history. In Africa alone, the number of Christians between 1950 and 1968 has risen from twenty million to fifty million. In Indonesia 400,000 have asked to be baptized in 1966 - 1969. And the growth continues. The chief need of the Indonesian Church (for exam-

[16] Amos 5:21-25.

ple, the Karo-Batak Church) is to find enough trained
workers to teach these masses of people basic Christian
doctrines and to help them become responsible Church
members.

The rapid growth of the Pentecostal churches in
Latin America is illustrative of the fact that suffering
from social injustice is by no means always an obstacle
to accepting a life of intensive piety. This is not a
justification of the inexcusable social situation in Latin
America. It does, however, question the thesis that the
suffering man asks the God-question only in terms of
bread and civil equality.

Why, then, the evangelicals rightly ask, is every
reference to the unique evangelistic opportunity absent
in the ecumenical study papers prepared for Uppsala
and in more recent publications? Why has no ecumenical missionary strategy been worked out in addition
to the social-revolutionary "opportunities for mission"
strategy which turns toward the special social tasks
in these areas of "opened doors"? The ecumenical concept of "mission" is defined as the total activity of the
Church oriented toward the world. But in this way,
are not those activities which have traditionally been
understood as "mission" neglected? Is not the original
theocentric dimension of this salvation overlooked when
one talks about salvation in a socio-ethical way as
"salvation for the whole man and his social situation"?

Any number of questions of this kind may be asked
in regard to the new "ecumenical" interpretation of
biblical-theological concepts. It is certainly helpful
that, in an ecumenical word-study of "conversion,"
the often-ignored social components have been exam-

ined in relation to conversion. [17] But, as L. Newbigin
has emphasized, it is less legitimate when the definition
of the total concept shrinks to a statement about its
consequences in the struggle for humanization. He
writes, "When St. Paul describes the fruit of his mission
at Thessalonica by saying: 'You turned from idols to
serve a living and true God and to wait for his Son
from heaven,' he did not refer to consequences of this
conversion which perhaps lay far beyond his imagina-
tion, but he described what he believed to be the
essential thing." [18]

In the biblical concept of conversion, the primary
concern is with that *new being* which is given by God.
The "ecumenicals," on the other hand, direct their
attention to the *functions* of conversion. This inclination toward exchanging biblical-ontological (related to
the being of God) thought for an inner-worldly func-
tional program corresponds to the contemporary metaphysical view of the world through the perspective of
the "one-dimensional man." [19] Theologically considered, the law is substituted for the Gospel. Therefore,
the "ecumenicals'" decisive need and challenge is to
discover again the New Testament priority of the in-
dicative of grace over the imperative of the new obedience.

Is there a theoretical possibility and a legitimate
hope that the evangelical and the "ecumenical" views

[17] Cf. E. Castro, "Conversion and Social Transformation," *Christian
Social Ethics in a Changing World,* John C. Bennett, ed., New York
(1967) pp. 348-66. E. R. Wickham, "Conversion in a Secular Age,"
Ecumenical Review (1967) pp. 291-96. *Drafts for Sections, Uppsala
68,* pp. 29, 36-37.

[18] L. Newbigin, "The Call to Mission — A Call to Unity?" *The
Church Crossing Frontiers* (cf. chapter 2, footnote 9) p. 262.

[19] H. Marcuse, *The One-Dimensional Man,* Boston (1964).

of mission can be reconciled in the correctives mentioned here?

The first aspect of this question must be differentiated from the second. The *theoretical* possibility does exist. At present, each conception has excluded a dimension which is radically developed in the other. The evangelical view of mission could come out of its socioethical *quietism* (introspection) if it dynamically integrated some of the basic intentions of the "ecumenical" view of history. And the "ecumenical" conception could break away from its *activism* in the world if, following the evangelical corrective, it could broaden its perspective eschatologically. It would then rediscover the sovereignty and the otherness of God's saving activity in the world.

Such an *integrated and total understanding of mission* is to be based on the biblical vision of a final salvation of a humanity which is united *with God* in Christ, in a completely whole world. It would radically diagnose man's socially broken condition in theological terms, i.e., as man's separation from God because of sin. Since this depraved condition destroys inter-personal relationships, a demonization of the social structures results. *Mission is, then, participation in the restoring, exorcising, and regenerating activity of the triune God.* This activity begins with the sending of His Son into the stream of history. It is continued *by confronting all human life with the offer of grace and the crucified and arisen One's claim of lordship* which transforms history. It achieves its goal in the culmination of history through the return of Christ in His visible Kingdom and finally through the creation of a new earth and a new heaven. Mission occurs, then, *primarily* in the proclamation of the redemptive act and of Jesus Christ's kingly lordship in all new and, as yet, untouched areas of life. It is *accompanied* by the authenticating presence of new life in the Spirit within the community of the Church, and by the transforming power of the Spirit in the believers, also in their obedient attempts to bring about better social structures.

Mission receives its dynamic by looking forward to the coming kingdom. In its perfect form, this kingdom is not a result of revolutionary changes or events in history which overcome everything except death and the power of sin; rather, it is seen eschatologically — as the new creation of God. This kingdom, however, now invisibly breaks into this transient world in those places where men, in faith, allow God's grace to work in them, and where they, in obedience, serve Him. The kingdom of God in anticipation already realizes itself within history in worship, in brotherhood, and in the application of the Gospel to the world.

Christ as the Lord of history guides history in such a way that one area of human life after another may be confronted with the Gospel. The Church's task in its mission is to take these situations seriously, whether it is accepting new ethnic groups for baptism or social crises which, when correctly mastered, contain the possibility for correcting old inadequate structures in a way appropriate to the Gospel. In both cases, mission occurs when — and only when — it is directed toward putting man's existence, through a conscious decision of faith, under Christ's lordship and His effective spiritual power. In this way, man experiences lasting salvation, a salvation in which his non-Christian environment may temporally participate.

But salvation in the full sense of the word is not found primarily in these indirect effects. Rather, salvation is the new communion of the Holy Spirit through the bond of peace. For this reason, the center of the missionary commission always remains its call into communion with Christ. This communion finds its visible representation and sacramental realization through responsible incorporation into the Church. The planting and growth of the Church as the body of Christ in the world remains the primary goal of mission within history. The transformation of the structures of this world is the result of a membership which is prepared to serve. This theological association of the primary Christocentric *being* and the world-oriented *function* arising from it, could, in principle, make possible a synthesis between the evangelical and the "ecumenical" understanding of mission.

WHERE IS THE ECUMENICAL MISSIONARY MOVEMENT BEING TAKEN?

Chapter V

WHERE IS THE ECUMENICAL MISSIONARY MOVEMENT BEING TAKEN?

In theory, a solution to the "ecumenical-evangelical" conflict seems conceivable. But what are the *real* chances for such a solution? This question cannot be answered on the basis of an objective theological analysis of both positions but rather only in the pursuit of the dynamic, advancing tendencies in both movements. We have mentioned that the evangelicals are basically ready to integrate the social dimension of the Gospel into their concept of mission. This means being basically ready to approach the issue; but it does *not* mean making a decision to join the World Council of Churches. The reason for their unwillingness to join the World Council is found not only in the continuing effect of traditional prejudices today but also in the shocking confrontation with the "horizontalistic" forces inside the ecumenical movement. To be sure, these forces represent neither the majority of Christians in the member churches nor of the General Assembly delegates. But in the fervor of their convictions radically minded officials and members of commissions and committees strongly influence the theological orientation and the strategy of the World Council.

At the beginning of the Fourth Assembly, Dr. W. A. Visser 'tHooft, in his important address on "The Mandate of the Ecumenical Movement," [1] expressly called for a reconciliation between the vertical and horizontal points of view: "A Christianity which has lost its vertical dimension has lost its salt and is not only insipid in itself, but useless for the world. But a Christianity which would use the vertical preoccupation as a means to escape from its responsibility for and in the common life of man is a denial of the incarnation, of God's love for the world manifested in Christ." [2]

This challenge represents the legacy of the retiring General Secretary of the World Council of Churches and was strongly emphasized in D. T. Niles' opening sermon [3] and in Prof. Berkhof's address on "The Finality of Jesus Christ." [4] Nevertheless, it was hardly heard in the deliberations of the sections — with the exception of the first. In reports about Section 2, the writers agree that the "verticalists" and the "horizontalists" had

---

[1] *The Uppsala Report 1968*, pp. 313-323.

[2] *Ibid.*, p. 318.

[3] "A crisis of faith has overtaken the churches more rigorously perhaps than ever before. Structures of church life and congregational worship are under serious questioning. The Bible has increasingly ceased to be a book to be listened to. It is asked whether even Jesus points beyond man to God." D. T. Niles, Opening Sermon: "Behold I make all things new," *Unity of Mankind*: Speeches from the Fourth Assembly of the World Council of Churches, Uppsala 1968, A. van den Heuvel, ed., Geneva (1969) p. 6.

[4] H. Berkhof, "The Finality of Jesus Christ," *The Uppsala Report 1968*, pp. 304-312.

shouted at each other over a deep abyss without having arrived at a mutual understanding. [5] The evangelicals were less responsible for this barrier in communication than were the "ecumenicals." The evangelicals were willing to listen. The English evangelical Rev. John R. W. Stott remarked, "The Assembly was preoccupied with the hunger, poverty and injustices of the contemporary world. I myself was deeply moved and challenged by it. I do not want to see it diminished. What worried me is that I found no comparable compassion or concern for the spiritual hunger of the unevangelized millions. . . . The Lord sent His Church to preach good news and make disciples, but I did not see the Assembly eager to obey this command of His. This same Lord wept over the unrepentant city which had rejected Him; but I did not see that Assembly weeping any similar tears." [6]

We can recognize the alarming depth of the present problem in the ecumenical movement's understanding of mission only when we also see it within the total context of the present *crisis of faith*, which has spread to the churches, as D. T. Niles pointed out in his opening sermon. It is not enough to say that failure to integrate the vertical dimension with the "ecumenical" understanding of mission is due only to a reaction against overemphasis on the vertical in the past. It is also found in the increasing inability of many people to conceive of the existence of a personal God. These

[5] Cf. John V. Taylor, *CMS Newsletter* (October, 1968). Also J. R. W. Stott: "But there was no real meeting of minds, no genuine dialogue, no apparent willingness to listen and understand as well as to speak and instruct." *Church Growth Bulletin* (November, 1968) p. 39.
[6] *Ibid.*

people appear unable to understand His spiritual reality which mysteriously breaks into their concrete lives, and they are equally unable to respond to His reality. When people become active missionaries in the evangelistic sense, their commitment comes from the spiritual event of their having been confronted by God in Christ. Because of this confrontation they feel a tremendous impetus to witness. This event cannot be replaced successfully by a legalistic reference to the Great Commission or by theologically explaining the logical relationship between the vertical and the horizontal dimensions. A church's evangelistic negligence always points out the weakness of its own spiritual life.

This argument cannot be completely refuted by the thesis that today the spiritual dynamic of the Church is found in another area of its total responsibility, namely, the socio-ethical. It is difficult to show where the social pathos, which presently involves so many Christians, is essentially different in foundation, appearance, and goal from the social pathos of contemporary humanistic and socialistic movements in general. Certainly, none of these movements can be understood apart from their origin in the world's having been confronted by Jesus Christ's prophetic message of salvation. [7] They have, however, lost sight of the message, and their goal seems to be a goal in history which is realized by men. The "ecumenicals," because of their theology of secularization, can no longer basically distinguish their concept of mission from other ideolog-

[7] Cf. L. Newbigin, "The Relevance of Trinitarian Doctrine for Today's Mission," CWME Study Pamphlets, No. 2, London (1963) pp. 35-51.

ically-motivated attempts to shape history. This is illustrated by the following central points:

1) The understanding of mission emerging from the
theology of secularization does not really want nor even
attempts to ground itself biblically. References to the
Bible are sporadic and arbitrary. The original meaning
of Scripture is distorted. The sociologists' empirical
analysis and the dialogue with those of other convictions are equally and strangely regarded to be sources
of understanding for missionary tasks and principles. [8]
Note the following quotation from the *Draft for Section I*:

> The contradiction becomes so great that some
> Christians look upon the processes of secular his-
> tory as furnishing new divine revelations which the
> churches must accept: they discern the activity of
> the Spirit in the emergence of free nations and in-
> ternational solidarities in undertakings where Chris-
> tians and non-Christians co-operate in seeking
> justice or peace in the new social structures created
> by the technical revolution. Such attitudes contest
> the claim that the Church alone is entrusted with
> the power to announce the kingdom of God and
> that its life and witness is the only true anticipa-
> tion of the Lord's coming. [9]

Here it is shown that in principle the basic, invariable "givenness" of the biblical message is surrendered

[8] "We are now witnessing a spate of literature on mission which,
even if quoting from the Bible, has either reversed or ignored at
least some of the biblical perspectives and priorities. The world's
agenda is being allowed to take precedence over the Bible's message,
and what the world says of itself is not being supplemented by what
the Bible says of the world." Canon D. Webster, "Bible and Mission:
Annual Sermon before the British and Foreign Bible Society, 9
March 1970," British and Foreign Bible Society (1970) p. 3.

[9] *Drafts for Sections*, "Section I," "The Holy Spirit and the Cath-
olicity of the Church," p. 10.

as a standard which judges and transcends all human understanding and all acts of God in history. We remember that in Barmen (1934), a *status confessionis* was declared when the uniqueness of that revelation in Jesus Christ seemed to be questioned by the Nazi-inspired theologians of the "German Christians." In Uppsala, this historic procedure was not followed, in spite of the fact that the previous New Delhi Assembly, because of pressure from the evangelicals, had accepted the phrase, "according to the Scriptures," as an addition to the basis of the World Council of Churches. The reference to the "Spirit" apart from the Word of Scripture is a typical characteristic of theological enthusiasm *(Schwärmertum)* which has now found equal status in the present *oikumene*. It will never give up this position freely.

2) The theological secularist exhibits just as little understanding of the spiritual essence of the Church of Jesus Christ as he does of the Bible. We notice in him the general tendency toward a conception of the Church as a purely sociological organization. He expects the Church to be renewed by adjusting to worldly structures. It can be shown that already the Dutch "Theology of the Apostolate" was so concerned with the *task* of the Church that it failed to consider her *essence* as an eschatological creation. This deficiency leads to a denial of the biblically indisputable fact that the Church is necessarily the temporary goal of mission. This denial also stems from another and similar fact: the theological secularist is unable to conceive of the sacramental and real presence of God both in the means of grace *(media salutis)* and in the community of saints — which, at the same time, is participation in the bless-

ings of salvation. This is illustrated by their equating the central Pauline doctrine of God's real presence with the heathen concept of Baal as a "residential god."

The inevitable result is the development of an increasingly open indifference to the congregation gathered around the Word and Sacraments. Indeed, Word and Sacrament are replaced by discussion and infor mation about current events, as exemplified in the "Political Evensong," a present experiment in secular worship, led by the "death of God" theologian Dorothee Sölle. [10]

3) Similarly, Uppsala illustrates the result of such one-dimensional thinking. Here "renewal in history" replaced the new heaven and the new earth of Revelation 21:1-5. The doctrine of a totally new creation is not fundamentally contested. This doctrine does, however, fade into the background when compared with the interest in revolutionary changes in history, which are accorded a Messianic place of honor. The inability rationally to see the promise of a new divine creation out of nothing leads one to reinterpret traditional eschatological terminology and let it serve to describe processes in history. The "de-sacralization" of salvation history leads to a "sacralization" of world history! [11]

The Puerto Rican theologian Justo González moves

[10] Examples are found in *Concept:* Arbeiten aus dem Referat für Fragen der Verkündigung, Special Issue 21 (German) pp. 14-17, where W. Hollenweger mentions Dorothee Sölle in the "Liturgy for Sunday."

[11] Per Lønning writes, "Putting a question mark behind a theology which sacralizes the secular as such (which in my opinion is what happens in a theology such as that of Cox-Hoekendijk-Hollenweger) does not mean to doubt the importance which is placed on social ethics at present by the ecumenical movement . . . ," *Kristen Gemenskap* (1968) quoted in *Norsk tidskrift for misjon* (1969) p. 36.

directly along this path to a "re-definition of the concept of sacrament." He would like to see the sacrament more strongly influenced by the "fundamental doctrine of the incarnation" which becomes for him the symbol of a general theology of history. The sacrament for him is "one of those historical instants, which God has chosen, in order to make himself known to us." González speaks of the "sacrament of service" as such a historical sacrament. This sacrament attempts to satisfy "the physical and social needs of our neighbor." [12]

For a belief which is based on the witness of Scripture and the Reformation, such an undertaking is wholly unacceptable. With reference to Harvey Cox's identification of the Kingdom of God with social change, W. Schmithals notes: "He who in his reflection on the New Testament allows man to be called to become the partner of God so that the Kingdom of God is established in an inner-worldly way, not only gives away 2,000 years of the Church's faith to heresy, but also takes the power away from the Gospel." [13]

The unqualified talk by the theology of secularization concerning "God's activity in history" intentionally fails to consider the important theological distinction involved in the question of whether such divine activity is done in providence, in grace, or in judgment. Here again we notice its typically deleterious characteristic of theological enthusiasm without theological precision.

In contrast to this, we must point out the correct

[12] Justo González, *Revolucion y encarnación Rio Piedras* (1965), quoted by C. Peter Wagner, *Latin American Theology:* Radical or Evangelical, pp. 40f.
[13] W. Schmithals, "Jesus und die Weltlichkeit des Reichs Gottes," *Evangelische Kommentare* (June, 1968) p. 319.

intention of the Lutheran distinction beween the two kingdoms of God — in spite of its one-sidedness. On the right, we find the Kingdom of Grace ruled by the Gospel and, on the left, the Kingdom of the hidden God ruled by the Law. It clearly recognizes that the powers of destruction (sin, death, and the devil) which govern throughout the Old Age, are not eliminated in history by human endeavors. It recognizes also that our salvation, notwithstanding its divine reality, is still a salvation in *hope*. To explain this radical, futuristic hope in the terms of the Marxist philosopher E. Bloch's *"Prinzip Hoffnung"* — *Principle of Hope* as a utopian vision within history, robs man of his true promises. When his historical utopias have finally been frustrated, he will be delivered over to radicalism or to despair.

4) In the "ecumenical" levelling of salvation history into secular history, *Christ*, to be sure, is still acclaimed as the real Author of salvation. Even here, however, one must carefully examine which understanding of Christ constitutes its basis. Practically all *Christological* formulas reappear in the pre-Uppsala documents. Three basic concepts, however, predominate:

First, Christ is understood as He who, through the eschatological dynamic of His proclamation, has initiated the processes of secularization and humanization in world history. [14]

[14] Cf. particularly the Jesus-sayings in the *Draft for Section 2, Drafts for Sections*, p. 28. Other examples: 1) "Our christology must begin with the Jew who makes it possible for us to share the hope of Israel, the hope for a kingdom of *Shalom*. . . . All Jesus does for Israel's hope is to universalize it, to make it available even to us *goyim*." Harvey Cox, *On Not Leaving It to the Snake*, SCM, London (1968) p. 18. 2) "The clear recognition that the leaven of the Gospel through the creation of the category of the *humanum* and through the basic revolutions of our time . . . in which modern man

Second, He is the One whose true humanity becomes the example for the humanization process today. [15]

Third, as the resurrected Lord of world history, He is the One who continually pushes this process of humanization forward until mankind is united in His humanity. [16]

In the first concept, Christ is the Creator of a central historical idea; in the second, He is the central existential Image within the progress of this history; in the third, He is the mythological legitimization (or supernaturally-based justification) of the Christian's involvement in a dynamic process within history — a history which, in reality, is interpreted according to its own inherent sociological laws and tendencies.

In all three instances, the "ecumenicals" use Christ to interpret and justify those socio-political processes

fights to realize new areas of human worth and to realize the promise of Christ for a comprehensive human life in these areas, has played a great role." M. M. Thomas, "Uppsala 1968 und die gegenwärtige theologische Lage," *Okumenische Rundschau* (1969) pp. 383 f.

[15] ". . . in this way Christ becomes the criterion for the humane, the saving power in the human struggle for humanity and the measure for a humanizing of the structures of life." M. M. Thomas, *Ibid.,* p. 384. Cf. also *The Church for Others,* p. 37: "This is a tremendous demand, and if we are to meet it we must have a new appreciation of Jesus as the Christ — of the Jew Jesus who was a real man and whose life corresponded completely to the will of God. In his identification with the world, the goal of God for both man and the world was expressed."

[16] Cf. W. Hollenweger, "Christus intra et extra muros ecclesiae," *Planning for Mission,* pp. 56-61. In addition, "The World in the Setting of Historical Change and Eschatological Hope," *Planning for Mission,* p. 75. M. M. Thomas, *Secular Man and Christian Mission,* P. Löffler, ed., p. 16. In the report as adopted by the Assembly (Section 2), "The Renewal in Mission," we read: "In the resurrection of Jesus a new creation was born, and the final goal of history was assured, when Christ as head of that new humanity will sum up all things." *The Uppsala Report 1968,* p. 28.

and decisions by which one participates in solidarity with humanists and Marxists. The latter arrive at the same results without this reference to Christ. Thus, out of these concepts evolves the new concept of the "Incognito-Christians" (those "believers" who do not directly confess their allegiance to Christ). And so, the revolutionary hero Che Guevara becomes the exemplary man who sacrificed himself for the Christian community. In these concepts, however, the biblical Christ is not truly expressed in His real message and His saving work. [17] In his critical review of Uppsala, E. Schlink rightly notes that the witness to Christ in the Assembly was weak in comparison to the analysis of the world situation or the guidance given for the Christian's engagement on behalf of justice and peace in the world: "Strangely enough, it remained a mere formula. It was taken for granted that Christ was called on, but the witness to Christ was not as predominant as the discussions of all the other themes; above all, the Word of the Cross was not the center of all statements. In the Section 2 report, more has been said concerning the 'how' of mission than concerning the contents of the missionary message." [18]

The trend in the affirmation leads one to suspect that the reference to Christ, even if it is the simple demand for a "personal relationship" to Him, [19] is merely a

[17] "Salvation Today," *Study Encounter 4* (1969). A. R. Tippett, in view of the concept of missions in the present World Student Christian Federation, speaks perceptively of their replacement of the incarnation of the Word by the idea of a "Christian presence" within the changes of history. *Verdict Theology in Missionary Theory*, Lincoln, Ill. (1969) p. 60.

[18] E. Schlink, "Der Heilige Geist und die Katholizität der Kirche," *Oekumenische Rundschau* (1969) p. 21.

[19] "Salvation Today," *Study Encounter 4* (1969).

theological tribute to that to which one as a Christian knows himself to be committed. This reference, however, can be extracted from the main concept without great difficulty. Does not Christ here simply fulfill the same ideological function as, for example, the idea of the class struggle in Karl Marx's left-Hegelian historical evolutionism? The true test of what one believes regarding the extent to which Christ functions in His sovereign lordship and purpose is found in what one has to say regarding the New Testament promise of His coming to judge at the end of history. But this apocalyptical statement — probably because it contradicts the idea of a humanity which will eventually be fully united in Christ — is either avoided or expressly rejected in publications by the theologians of secularization. [20]

5) This brings us to the worst consequence which could arise if one carried this line of thinking further: Does not this new missionary concept of the theology of secularization encourage the presupposition of the "death of God theology," namely, that humanity itself can deal with its own history, even *without God's* transcendental intervention and, finally, even without a direct reference to Him? To be sure, one still speaks of God, but without really taking His explicit demands and promises and His nature as revealed in salvation history seriously. M. L. Kretzmann notes that the word "God" is used in a light and careless way, as if, in

[20] "Can we set aside both falling firmament and sprouting spores as our images of history and act on the conviction that there is no future except the one we make?" Harvey Cox, *On Not Leaving It to the Snake,* p. 46.

regard to the needs of the world, He were an unknown factor in mission. [21]

The most frightening feature of this theological development in the World Council in general, and in the Division for World Mission and Evangelism in particular, is the express *attempt* to substitute *man* for *God*. Nowhere is this so vividly expressed as in the new definition of the goal of mission which first appeared in the report, "The Church for Others" [22] and which was later accepted in the commentary to the Geneva Draft for Section 2.

> We have lifted up humanization as the goal of mission because we believe that more than other [positions] it communicates in our period of history the meaning of the messianic goal. In another time the goal of God's redemptive work might best have been described in terms of man turning towards God. . . . The fundamental question was that of the true God, and the Church responded to that question by pointing to Him. It was assuming that the purpose of mission was Christianization, bringing man to God through Christ and His Church. Today the fundamental question is much more that of *true man*, and the dominant concern of the missionary congregation must therefore be to point to the humanity in Christ as the goal of mission. [23]

One reads, is startled — and reads once more. With this programmatic declaration, Paul's central question of how man may be justified before God and may have

[21] M. L. Kretzmann, "Cross-Currents in Mission," *Department for World Missions Newsletter of the Lutheran World Federation*, 35 (June, 1969) p. 8.

[22] In the report of the North American study group "The Church for the World," *The Church for Others*, p. 78.

[23] *Drafts for Sections, The Uppsala Report 1968*, p. 34.

· communion with Him becomes an obsolete concern. This concern is not merely supplemented by the question about man and his relationship to his fellowman; it is replaced by it.

The Latin-American theologian Gonzalo Castillo Cardenas argued along the same lines at the Geneva Conference for Church and Society (1966). There is, he argued, a deep tension between two present types of theologies. "One, centered in God, the other centered in man; one integrist and separatist in relation to society in general, the other committed to society as a whole; one attached to dogmatic principles and structures of traditional Christianity, the other committed only to the man, in the particular situation. In the words of Teilhard de Chardin: 'Around us the real struggle does not take place between believers and unbelievers, but between two kinds of believers, two ideals, two concepts of God. A religion of the earth is being formed against the religion of Heaven.'" [24]

This radical displacement of the center from God to man and the replacement of theology by anthropology is not a painful slip by some extremists of the theology of secularization. Rather, it has become the declared program according to such key figures in the World Council of Churches as Mr. M. M. Thomas, who in Uppsala was elected the new chairman of the central committee. At the beginning of the Uppsala Conference, he gave a report on "Issues Concerning the Life and Work of the Church in a Revolutionary World." In this address he clearly defined the goal of the Fourth Assembly as well as the future course of

[24] "Christians and the Struggle for a New Social Order in Latin America," (mimeographed paper) Geneva (1966).

the World Council in terms of the work and the results of the Geneva Conference for Church and Society. [25]

"It seems to me," Mr. Thomas said, "that the significance of the conference for the churches lies precisely in that it has the potentiality of bringing them to awareness of the radical changes taking place in men's relations to nature and to their fellowmen through the technical and social revolutions of our time and of the spiritual depth of the revolution in religious self-understanding which has taken place in man himself. And the impact of it all on the theological leadership of the churches and the ecumenical movement shows that the conference's focus on the human and the human situation has become the turning point for ecumenical service, unity worship, and all aspects of the being and ministry of the Church." [26]

This "focus on the human and the human situation" appears to me to be the crucial — in fact, the disastrous — turning point in the present course of the ecumenical movement. This new focus logically corresponds to a conscious and definite turning away from God as the absolute and ultimate Reference-Point for all Christian thought and service. In contrast to this, the Bible and all the confessions of the various churches maintain that the glorification of God's name and His saving acts are the highest purpose of man. Even the soteriological aspect of man's salvation is subordinated to this. Without doxology as the beginning and the end of all Christian statements, man's salvation becomes self-salvation; man puts himself ultimately in the place of God.

[25] M. M. Thomas, "Issues Concerning the Life and Work of the Church in a Revolutionary World," van den Heuvel, p. 83.

[26] Ibid., p. 89.

The agonizing question for me is whether such a re-directing of the focus from God to man, in other words, from doxology to man's relationship to his fellowman (even as a temporary program of Church action to re-inforce in our time the Great Commandment, "Love your brother!"), is possible, without anti-Christian symptoms being finally developed and thus increasing-ly turning *against* God.

For several months, we have observed with growing apprehension these tendencies in the public activities of youth involved in social revolution. Special com-mittees composed of Protestant and Roman Catholic theological students have been formed as pressure groups. They have produced and distributed leaflets and undertaken provocative activities which actually have a blasphemic character. At the 1969 *Kirchentag* in Stuttgart, placards which ridiculed some of the cen-tral statements of the Creed were carried and dis-played before thousands of Christians.

This is not just a typical German phenomenon. Sim-ilar developments are also found in the central meetings of the World Student Christian Federation, which for many decades was the World Council of Churches' "main recruiting pool," as William Temple called it. The report of the Rev. Ø. Thelle, a Norwegian student pastor, [27] lies before me. Mr. Thelle was a delegate to the World Student Conference (July, 1968) in Turku, Finland. Three hundred and fifty students from all over the world assembled there. One of his colleagues was

[27] "Babel's forvirring og/eller politisk pinseunder?" (Babel's Con-fusion or the Political Miracle of Pentecost?) *Ekumenisk Orientering* (September, 1968) pp. 7f. Pastor Øystein Thelle is National Secre-tary for the Christian Student World Federation in Norway.

jeered by the full assembly and drowned out with demonstrative calls of "Hallelujah" and "Amen" just because he attempted to say something positive about the "proclamation of the Gospel." [28]

There may still be people who tend to evaluate such outbreaks as expressions of a temporary fermentative process in the youth. Personally, when faced with the blatant abandonment of genuine biblical concern, I find it difficult to see the likelihood of a return to the substance of Christian faith. But is there also a justification for the new development in which, even in the publications of the Geneva Division for World Mission and Evangelism, the biblical contents of faith are openly repressed by a contemporary anthropocentric reinterpretation? For example, two well-known members of the Geneva staff have "translated," [29] with a shockingly alienating effect, the narrative of Jesus' birth into the present revolutionary situation. In the "Monthly Letter about Evangelism," [30] we read: "While some Christians were commemorating the twenty-century-old Calvary of Christ in their churches, young Christians and non-Christians . . . commemorated the calvary of Man who bears the cross of physical and spiritual Hunger. In Christian terms this means: New forms of worship in a secularized world." (In the German trans-

[28] In regard to the Christian presence idea in the World Student Christian Federation in the U.S.A., A. Glasser reports, "These men appear solely concerned with radical social reform, even violent revolution. They are frequently hostile to the evangelistic mandate." "Confession, Church Growth and Authentic Unity in Missionary Strategy," N. A. Horner, *op. cit.* (Cf. chapter 2, footnote 1) p. 191.

[29] "Bethlehem heute," *Der Gärtner* 2 (December 1, 1969).

[30] No. 617, June/September, 1963, p. 3; Edisson H. Osorio, "Is Fasting a Form of Evangelism? A Symbolic Action and Its Interpretation in Puerto Rico."

lation, the word "*Anbetung*," which actually means "adoration," is used here for "worship.")

Looking back at the International Missionary Council meeting in Ghana (1958), Walter Freytag wrote that today one has the impression that "something like a new religion has developed" from the decay and the transformation of the old Asian religions. [31] "All religions and anti-religions are transcended, and merged into one single religion — the world religion of the gods of this world. That which here is called gods has a Christian origin. These gods, however, are cut loose from their source. Without Christ, they have become independent. Nations serve them and place their hope in them, leaving God aside."

Freytag wrote this in the light of the renascent eastern religions. In view of this he wanted to call the Christian mission to a new Christocentric witness. When we read his remarks ten years later, we are shocked by the present observation that this same syncretistic movement has silently begun to change Christianity, the churches, the ecumenical movement, and even the Christian mission itself! Is there not a similarity to the understanding of Christian mission by the theology of secularization when Freytag writes, "One finds the same vocabulary in their proclamation everywhere. Peace, freedom, tolerance, and social justice are the main words. They are not only moral slogans. . . . They also have a messianic ring and proclaim that future which man forms, the 'better life' with all that is included in it — standard of living, security, freedom from want, and a new political reality." [32]

[31] W. Freytag, "Nach Ghana," *Reden und Aufsätze*, Part I, p. 123.
[32] *Ibid.*, p. 122.

Today the Christian mission is told to set out for the ideological World Market with similar offerings. It must do this by using a few catch-words, such as "*shalom*" and "new humanity." The content, however, is the same as that of the secularist's vocabulary. The question is whether there is a need for Christian missions at all. If one has nothing to offer other than that which all others with the same missionary drive also offer, he has basically become superfluous. Here a judgment applies to the Christian mission which must sound terrible to all Christians even though they know that as witnesses they may expect to suffer martyrdom: "Go away, you have become unnecessary." [33]

We have asked about the *tendencies* on which the real claim for synthesis between the evangelical and ecumenical missionary movements depends—a synthesis which might be theoretically conceivable. The actual result, however, is doubtful. On the ecumenical side, we see ideological forces at work which threaten to pervert everything positive in an aroused Christian responsibility for the suffering world into that which is pseudo-messianic. Fortunately, in Uppsala these forces were not able to drive their way through. But their fascinating dynamic is still there and it extends into their ecumenical progeny. The conservative evangelicals are aware of this danger. For many of them, "Uppsala only served to confirm their darkest thoughts of the Ecumenical Movement." [34] The prospects then for reaching an understanding in the near future are not promising.

[33] H. U. von Balthaser, *Cordula oder der Ernstfall*, Einsiedeln (1966) p. 113.
[34] A. Glasser, *Evangelical Missions Quarterly* (1969) p. 137.

Still it would be unfortunate for *both sides* to discontinue the dialogue which is so urgently desired by many men in the World Council. By abandoning dialogue, the evangelical movement might purchase the rescue of its evangelical missionary concern with the price of a proper view of the Church, ecumenical unity, and perhaps also of witness in matters of state and society. On the other hand, the mission of the World Council of Churches, with its factual renunciation of saving proclamation, would fall even more deeply into a purely this-world-oriented, socio-ethical (or revolutionary) movement. At the end they could await Dostoevski's Grand Inquisitor or even Solovev's Anti-Christ.

The situation is threatening enough. At the 1968 "Conference for World-Wide Cooperation in Questions of Development," convened by the World Council of Churches and the Papal Commission for Justice and Peace, outstanding experts from all confessions and denominations defined the function of Christian mission as "aid for development." They stated that "the missionary societies should be encouraged to place the work for justice and development in the center of their activity." For the hope and the future of the world is found in the development of earthly riches for the general good of humanity. Indeed, the hope for development is, in the judgment of the Beirut Conference, "the basic hope of man." [35]

It is alarming to learn that only with the utmost

[35] *Weltentwicklung, die Herausforderung an die Kirchen:* Konferenz für weltweite Zusammenarbeit in Entwicklungsfragen, 21-27 April, 1968, Beirut (Lebanon), edited by the Committee for Society, Development, and Peace, Geneva (1968) 55; 17. Cf. also p. 20: "We find our true humanity while working with others for the changing of obsolete structures and the creation of new wealths."

efforts of the evangelical delegates and through such authorities as Lesslie Newbigin, the former Director of the Division for World Mission, and Donald Coggan, the Anglican Archbishop of York, was it possible to insert elementary references to the importance of biblical teaching into the final report of Uppsala's Section 2 and as the necessity of new birth or the need for Scripture study to vivify missionary awareness in the local congregation. [36]

In the light of the approaching Conference on World Mission to be held in Indonesia in 1972, these experiences underline in an alarming way the need for current efforts on the part of Geneva to integrate the ecumenical socio-ethical concerns and the evangelical soteriological concerns in a harmonious manner. Both sides must be willing to listen to each other and even to repent. The main concern is not, as a Geneva preparatory document disarmingly suggested, simply the connection between "personal salvation and social justice." [37] It is not a simple relation between the individual and society which ultimately must be determined, but rather the question about the lasting validity of the biblical Gospel as that certain and binding Self-disclosure of the triune God.

[36] According to J. R. W. Stott, *Church Growth Bulletin* (November, 1969) p. 38.

[37] "Salvation Today" (mimeographed paper) edited by the World Council of Churches, Division for World Missions 56/68/(G), p. 6.

IMPLICATIONS FOR THE
GERMAN EVANGELICAL MISSION

Chapter VI

IMPLICATIONS FOR THE
GERMAN EVANGELICAL MISSION

What consequences arise from this analysis of the conflict between the "ecumenical" and the "evangelical" wings of the International Missionary Movement for German Protestants? It should now be clear that the main question here is not that of two widely divergent groups which are foreign to or suspicious of us in their particular traditions of piety and their world view. The questions asked here are very basic, for they concern the center of our own faith as well as the basis and goal of that activity to which we have been called. In fact, we are dealing here with an ecumenical actualization of those very questions which our own congregations, synods, councils, and training institutes are also asking with increasing frequency.

Following a lively discussion, the societies involved in the German Missionary Council (1960) resolved by majority vote, to support the resolution drawn up in Ghana. This resolution affirms the International Missionary Council's merger with the World Council of Churches. [1] The resolution was accepted in the belief that it would be a step of obedience in the divine movement of Church and mission toward a world-wide unity. This acceptance was also made in the hope that in the future both missionary and the evangelistic concerns would be considered by the larger, unified World Council. At the same time, the German evangelical missions assumed co-responsibility for the spiritual course of the ecumenically integrated World Missionary Movement.

Thus when we note that, from the beginning of the preparation for the Fourth General Assembly, the Division for World Mission and Evangelism seems to have been listening to those voices which contradict the goals worked out and supported by all the earlier World Missionary Conferences, we cannot allow ourselves to be unconcerned. As John Stott rightly noted, it is a breach of trust. We cannot simply, in an ecumenical euphoria, accept and support everything which comes to us out of the World Council of Churches as being directed by the Holy Spirit. Luther's famous statement is still valid today: "Pope and councils can also err." Actually, the Germans and Scandinavians had made several corrective or alternative statements in regard to the Fourth Assembly. These statements have, however, received only indirect and limited attention. We cannot be satisfied with the fact that the original draft for Section 2, which was so strongly in-

[1] *Evangelische Missions-Zeitschrift* (1958) pp. 187f.; (1960) pp. 186-88.

fluenced by the theology of secularization, was replaced by a theologically ambiguous one in Uppsala. The question to be asked is this: What elements will eventually arise from this syncretistic section report in the face of those active forces in the *oikumene* which have determined its development between the Third and the Fourth Assemblies? Under the banner of the growing movement for "Church and Society," they will in all likelihood direct the course of the *oikumene* in the future even more strongly.

I would like especially to emphasize my feeling that the present openness of the churches to the Third World's urgent socio-political problems is legitimate and in keeping with the goals of the earlier Movement for Life and Work. Insofar as the churches do their best to assert Jesus' command of brotherly love in global dimensions and in the categories of justice, peace, and the dignity of man, they deserve our active support — morally and materially. Obviously even the work of mission cannot be conducted apart from those new forms of ecumenical assistance for the areas of their own traditional activity. A new concept of mission must be developed in which its specific tasks are combined with the broader total responsibility of the Church to the nations of the Third World.

But, at the same time, facing the threatening danger that the ecumenical social responsibility may come under a false ideological or even pseudo-messianic sign, we are called to withstand such voices and tendencies. Mission is called to do this in a unique way. Its specific task within the total activity of the Church is to be the spearhead of God's turning to the world. It does this by testifying to the center of the Gospel which must

be proclaimed. Here the main concern is first and fore-
most that men receive eternal salvation. At its nucleus,
this salvation is independent of all historical and cultural conditions and it is the same for every man and
every age, i.e., the forgiveness of sins and the acceptance into living community with Jesus.

Today mission must accomplish many subsidiary
tasks which are a part of the preparation, support,
authentication, and consequence of its message. These
ancillary tasks can also have eschatological significance,
but they receive this significance only from the soteriological center of the Gospel. This center is uniquely
entrusted to the missionary. It is, therefore, important
that he is not lost in those subsidiary activities which
are the main topic of conversation today. Proclamation,
the intention and hope of which is conversion, baptism,
and church membership, must again become his basic
activity. [2] The Second Vatican Council's decree of Mission, "Ad Gentes," shows that this is no antiquated
understanding. It defines the central task of mission as
follows: "Finis proprius activitatis huius missionalis est
evangelizatio et plantatio Ecclesiae in populis vel coe-
libus in quibus nondum radicata est" (I, 6). [3] (The
true purpose of the missionary enterprise is evangelization and the establishment of the Church among peoples and in places where it has not yet taken root.)

The German Protestant mission ought not support
theologically a concept of "mission" which is distorted
or which, through a pan-missionary inflation, has lost

[2] Cf. G. F. Vicedom, Die Mission am Scheideweg, Berlin (1967)
pp. 16 f., 73. Also Mission in einer Welt der Revolution, Wuppertal
(1969) p. 55.
[3] J. Glazik, ed., Zweites Vatikanisches Konzil: Dekret über die
Missionstätigkeit der Kirche, Münster (1967) p. 44.

44209

its *proprium* and thereby also its impetus. The words of Walter Freytag ought to be remembered here: "Nothing can be called mission in the biblical sense which is not . . . directed toward conversion and baptism." [4]

All this has far-reaching consequences for the shaping of our own missionary activity. For the majority of our missionary societies, inter-church aid has slowly replaced true mission during the post-war decades. Little objection can be raised when the missionary societies, to a limited degree, also participate in these services. Their workers, however, ought to be continually reminded that their primary mission is to win new people to Christ.

Missionaries ought to transmit this same apostolic consciousness to those congregations and churches from which and to which they are sent. If the slogan "Church for Others" has meaning at all, it means that the Church is not merely called to maintain the existing congregations, but rather it is responsible for that humanity which has not been reached or is no longer being reached by the Gospel. The concern both for the eternal salvation and the temporal well-being of others is a part of this and in precisely that order. This must have consequences for a new distribution of the financial means of the Church, especially in view of

[4] W. Freytag, "Zwischenkirchliche Hilfe und Internationaler Missionsrat," *Reden und Aufsätze*, Part II, p. 85. Cf. H. Lindsell: "But to bring all that the Church is supposed to do under the term 'mission' is to do semantic violence to a good term and to divest it of a significance it has always had." "Missionary Imperatives: A Conservative Evangelical Exposition," *Protestant Cross-Currents in Mission:* The Ecumenical-Conservative Encounter, Norman A. Horner, ed., Nashville, Abingdon Press (1968) p. 53.

her new commitment to give aid to underdeveloped countries.

Finally, and this is the most important consequence, our mission societies must acquire insight as to how we can concretely help direct the course of the Commission and Division for World Mission and Evangelism in a responsible theological direction. If we do not do this, we are also responsible for the spiritual fate of those two billion people who, at present, are outside the specific interests of this Division. As the social anthropologists emphasize, the whole animistic world presently finds itself involved in a crucial historical phase of cultural upheaval. [5] Millions of Africans and Asians today are put in the position of having to decide whether they ought to exchange their traditional religion for Islam, Christianity, communism, or a nativistic new religion. The fullness of time has *now* come for the animistic bloc. World missions stands on the threshold of unique opportunities of which the younger churches cannot take advantage alone. The individualistic operation of pioneer-minded missionary societies can often hurt just as much as help. The present situation, as never before, calls for a co-ordinated international strategy of mission. The ecumenical Commission for World Mission and Evangelism is called upon to

[5] Cf. E. de Vries, *Man in Rapid Social Change*, London (1961) p. 232. Cf. also A. R. Tippett (Professor of Missionary Anthropology) "For Uppsala to consider," *Church Growth Bulletin*, Vol. IV, 5 (May, 1968) p. 10. "The authors (of the draft for Section 2 in Uppsala) seem to have been quite unaware of one fact of global significance — that the great animist world is 'turning over' like an iceberg in our day, and taking up a new position, which may be a determinative factor in world history for the next century. Whether we like it or not, millions of people are changing from something old to something new. . . ."

provide leadership for one such common strategy. Ought we not give much more support to determined attempts such as that of Alan Walker? Mr. Walker, who is the superintendent of the Central Methodist Mission in Sydney, Australia, once in New Delhi (1961) and again in Uppsala (1968), supported by the Australian Council of Churches, appealed to the World Council to call its member churches to a "world-wide Christian mission." Both times he failed! [6]

Along with such strategic considerations goes the more important *theological* concern. The threat of the perversion of the biblical understanding of mission as well as of the Christian faith must not be viewed fatalistically. This threat is not alleviated by the fact that in our own churches we are engaged in exactly the same theological discussion in regard to the existence and the non-existence of the Christian confession. Many missionary societies, thanks to that stream of tradition which bears them, to their charismatic independence in contrast to the institutional churches, and to their direct relationship to a spiritually alive congregation, have always been able to protect themselves, by a certain inner immunity, from the current ideological infections of their supporting churches. Insofar as they do this today, they ought to be able to ascertain point for point to what extent they must judge the above-mentioned theological tendencies in the *oikumene* as dangerous, false doctrines which are to be resisted.

A forceful attempt in this direction is the "Frankfurt Declaration on the Fundamental Crisis in Christian Missions," which was issued by a well-known group of confession-minded German theologians in March,

[6] J. R. W. Stott, *Church of England Newspaper* (August 23, 1968).

1970. It is the German counterpart to the Wheaton Declaration. On the basis of this declaration, the Commission should be induced to listen to the objections and to answer them in a responsible way. If the document is well-supported by many signers from all churches and missions, it could lead to a decisive theological re-orientation and a correspondingly new arrangement in the working program for the Geneva Division and its regional councils.

In describing our missionary tasks and goals, it is certainly not enough today merely to repeat the formulations of earlier missionary conferences. The discovery of the significance of social and ecclesiastical structures associated with the proper delivery of the missionary message today has caused those structures to become a legitimate concern for the Commission for World Mission and Evangelism and we must incorporate them into our present understanding of mission. But we must convincingly express anew our unchangeable conviction that mission is a kerygmatic, sacramental, and diaconal presentation of eternal salvation. This salvation is, once and for all, grounded in God's great saving act in Christ. It comes into the world only through that apostolic proclamation which was instituted by Christ Himself. Only its radiation through men, who themselves are reconciled and, therefore, are agents of reconciliation, makes changes in structure meaningful. Only in attaining this salvation can man find his true *humanity*. This humanity is found in the God-likeness promised to him, i.e., in his being the image-bearer and the child of God, a participant in His kingdom now and in the coming world.

THE FRANKFURT DECLARATION

Appendix

THE FRANKFURT DECLARATION

An Introductory Statement

"Woe to me if I do not preach the Gospel!" (1 Cor. 9:16, rsv)

A most heartening missionary document has recently come out of Germany. The Frankfurt Declaration addresses itself to the fundamental crisis in Christian missions and on a clear biblical basis calls Christians, churches, and missionary societies back to their God-given task. Dr. Donald McGavran, dean of the School of World Mission at Fuller Theological Seminary, describes the background of the declaration and urges American readers to respond:

Dr. Peter Beyerhaus, author with Henry Lefever of *The Responsible Church and the Foreign Mission* and director of the Institute of the Discipline of Missions and Ecumenical Theology of the University of Tübingen in Germany, has been greatly disturbed at the humanistic turn that World Council of Churches missions have taken. Feeling that the Uppsala statement on missions was no mere surface ripple but signaled a profound change of direction, he wrote *Humanisierung — Einzige Hoffnung Der Welt?* ("humanization — the only hope of the world?"). As soon as I read it, I wrote Dr. Beyerhaus about publication of the work in English. I also urged him to gather German theologians of like precious faith and issue a declaration calling Christians and churches to a thoroughly sound and Christian concept of mission. Dr. Beyerhaus replied:

> You will be interested to hear that in German churches and missionary societies a deep unrest caused by the present departure from what we believe to be the genuine motives and goals of missions has developed. It is similar to the unrest which led to the appearance of the Wheaton Declaration. I was asked by an association of confession-minded theologians, "The Theological Convention," to write a first draft for such a declaration. This paper was discussed thoroughly at our meeting on 4 March 1970 in Frankfurt and at the end unanimously accepted after slight revisions. It is now being printed in several German publications, and invitations for signatures have been sent to persons in key positions. Many have already responded positively.
>
> Knowing your vital concern for the upholding of a clear biblical motivation and practice of mission, I am sure you will rejoice in this venture. We have now prepared an English translation which will serve as a basis for deliberations with missionary leaders on an international level. Perhaps American theologians will be interested to join our German adventure.

Among the first signers of the Frankfurt Declaration are:

Professor P. Beyerhaus, Th.D., Tübingen
Professor W. Böld, Th.D., Saarbrücken

Professor E. Ellwein, Th.D., Erlanger
Professor H. Engelland, Th.D., Kiel
Professor H. Frey, Th.D., Bethel
Professor J. Heubach, Th.D., Lauenburg
Herr Dr. A. Kimme, Th.D., Leipzig
Professor W. Künneth, Th.D., Ph.D., D.D., Erlangen
Professor O. Michel, Th.D., Tübingen
Professor W. Mundle, Th.D., Marburg
Professor H. Rohrbach, Ph.D., Mainz
Professor G. Stählin, Th.D., Mainz
Professor G. Vicedom, Th.D., D.D., Neuendettelsau
Professor U. Wickert, Th.D., Tübingen
Professor J. W. Winterhager, Th.D., Berlin

Signatures are pouring in to Dr. Beyerhaus. On May 11 he wrote me again, saying, "The declaration has stirred up commotion in the whole German-speaking missionary world. The reaction differs between enthusiastic support and passionate rejection! But the supporters seem to be in the majority."

The official English translation has just reached me, and I make haste to share it with Christians in North America. Although it arose quite independently, like the Wheaton Declaration (published in *The Church's Worldwide Mission,* edited by Harold Lindsell, Word, 1966) it speaks to "a fundamental crisis" in missions. It is a tremendous pronouncement issued to "clarify the true missionary motives and goals of the Church of Jesus Christ." It rings true to the Bible. It rings true to historic missions. It will cheer all those engaged in world evangelization and confound the enemies of the Gospel.

In Germany most missionary societies are aligned

with the World Council of Churches. In the Frankfurt Declaration, the conservative elements in the churches appeal to Geneva to reverse its stand that horizontal reconciliation is the only suitable mission strategy for our day. How far Geneva will yield remains to be seen.

In North America many churches are similarly aligned with the World Council of Churches. Indeed, since they are also aligned with the National Council of Churches, they are somewhat to the left of Europe's churches. The Frankfurt Declaration gives the conservative elements in each church (the silent majority?) a chance to appoint someone to receive signatures and to flood denominational headquarters with them, demanding emphasis on vertical reconciliation.

However, in North America many churches and many congregations and hundreds of thousands of individuals are unaligned with the World Council of Churches and the National Council of Churches. They are already sending abroad more than twenty thousand missionaries through societies holding substantially the position of the Frankfurt Declaration. They may deal with the statement in one of two ways:

1. Watch what happens within the WCC-NCC aligned bodies.

2. Declare themselves in favor of the biblical position taken by these confession-minded German theologians and missiologists. I would like to see every missionary society of the Evangelical Foreign Missions Association and the Interdenominational Foreign Mission Association plus independent missionary societies by the score promptly signing the declaration and making it known that "this defines our unshakable position on mission.

If you want to do this kind of missions, do it through us."

In view of the multiform nature of the missionary societies of North America—their many denominational affiliations, alliances, shades of theological opinion, sources of income, and types of work — I cannot suggest that readers send signatures to any common address. But those who agree with the statement should joyfully stand up and be counted. This is a time to act, a widespread signing of the Frankfurt Declaration by theologians and missionary-minded Christians is in order. Readers will know where to send signatures — probably to missionary societies or to denominational headquarters. Let each tell his or her missionary society or church that he believes in this kind of mission and will support it.

Let us keep pace with our fellow Christians in Germany. Two months from now, may we, like Professor Beyerhaus, be able to say: "The reaction differs between enthusiastic support and passionate rejection, but the supporters seem to be in the majority."

from *Christianity Today*

TEXT OF THE DECLARATION

The Church of Jesus Christ has the sacred privilege and irrevocable obligation to participate in the mission of the triune God, a mission which must extend into all the world. Through the Church's outreach, his name shall be glorified among all people, mankind shall be saved from his future wrath and led to a new life, and the lordship of his Son Jesus Christ shall be established in the expectation of his second coming.

This is the way that Christianity has always understood the Great Commission of Christ, though, we must confess, not always with the same degree of fidelity and clarity. The recognition of the task and the total missionary obligation of the Church led to the endeavor to integrate missions into the German Protestant churches and the World Council of Churches, whose Commission and Division of World Mission and Evangelism was established in 1961. It is the goal of this division, by the terms of its constitution, to insure "the proclamation to the whole world of the Gospel of Jesus Christ, to the end that all men may believe in him and be saved." It is our conviction that this definition reflects the basic apostolic concern of the New Testament and restores the understanding of mission held by the fathers of the Protestant missionary movement.

Today, however, organized Christian world missions is shaken by a fundamental crisis. Outer opposition and the weakening spiritual power of our churches and missionary societies are not solely to blame. More dangerous is the displacement of their primary tasks by means of an insidious falsification of their motives and goals.

Deeply concerned because of their inner decay, we feel called upon to make the following declaration.

We address ourselves to all Christians who know themselves through the belief in salvation through Jesus Christ to be responsible for the continuation of his saving work among nonchristian people. We address ourselves further to the leaders of churches and congregations, to whom the worldwide perspective of their spiritual commission has been revealed. We address ourselves finally to all missionary societies and their coordinating agencies, which are especially called, accord-

ing to their spiritual tradition, to oversee the true goals
of missionary activity.

We urgently and sincerely request you to test the following theses on the basis of their biblical foundations,
and to determine the accuracy of this description of the
current situation with respect to the errors and modes
of operation which are increasingly evident in churches,
missions, and the ecumenical movement. In the event
of your concurrence, we request that you declare this
by your signature and join with us in your own sphere
of influence, both repentant and resolved to insist upon
these guiding principles.

Seven Indispensable Basic Elements of Mission

1   *Full authority in heaven and on earth has been
    committed to me. Go forth therefore and make all
    nations my disciples; baptize men everywhere in
    the name of the Father and the Son and the Holy
    Spirit, and teach them to observe all that I have
    commanded you. And be assured, I am with you
    always, to the end of time (Matt. 28:18-20; this
    Scripture quotation and those that follow are from
    the New English Bible).*

We recognize and declare:

Christian mission discovers its foundation, goals,
tasks, and the content of its proclamation solely in the
commission of the resurrected Lord Jesus Christ and his
saving acts as they are reported by the witness of the
apostles and early Christianity in the New Testament.
Mission is grounded in the nature of the Gospel.

We therefore oppose the current tendency to determine the nature and task of mission by socio-political

analyses of our time and from the demands of the non-christian world. We deny that what the Gospel has to say to people today at the deepest level is not evident before its encounter with them. Rather, according to the apostolic witness, the Gospel is normative and given once for all. The situation of encounter contributes only new aspects in the application of the Gospel. The surrender of the Bible as our primary frame of reference leads to the shapelessness of mission and a confusion of the task of mission with a general idea of responsibility for the world.

2   *Thus will I prove myself great and holy and make myself known to many nations; they shall know that I am the Lord (Ezek. 38:23).*
Therefore, Lord, I will praise thee among the nations and sing psalms to thy name (Ps. 18:49 and Rom. 15:9).

We recognize and declare:

The first and supreme goal of mission is the *glorification* of the name of the one *God* throughout the entire world and the proclamation of the lordship of Jesus Christ, his Son.

We therefore oppose the assertion that mission today is no longer so concerned with the disclosure of God as with the manifestation of a new man and the extension of a new humanity into all social realms. *Humanization* is not the primary goal of mission. It is rather a product of our new birth through God's saving activity in Christ within us, or an indirect result of the Christian proclamation in its power to perform a leavening activity in the course of world history.

A one-sided outreach of missionary interest toward man and his society leads to atheism.

3   *There is no salvation in anyone else at all, for there is no other name under heaven granted to men, by which we may receive salvation (Acts 4:12).*

We recognize and declare:

Jesus Christ our Saviour, true God and true man, as the Bible proclaims him in his personal mystery and his saving work, is the basis, content, and authority of our mission. It is the goal of this mission to make known to all people in all walks of life the gift of his salvation.

We therefore challenge all nonchristians, who belong to God on the basis of creation, to believe in him and to be baptized in his name, for in him alone is eternal salvation promised to them.

We therefore oppose the false teaching (which is spreading in the ecumenical movement since the Third General Assembly of the World Council of Churches in New Delhi) that Christ himself is anonymously so evident in world religions, historical changes, and revolutions that man can encounter him and find salvation in him without the direct news of the Gospel.

We likewise reject the unbiblical limitation of the person and work of Jesus to his humanity and ethical example. In such an idea the uniqueness of Christ and the Gospel is abandoned in favor of a humanitarian principle which others might also find in other religions and ideologies.

4   *God loved the world so much that he gave his only Son, that everyone who has faith in him may not die but have eternal life (John 3:16).*

In Christ's name, we implore you, be reconciled to God (II Cor. 5:20).

We recognize and declare:

Mission is the witness and presentation of eternal salvation performed in the name of Jesus Christ by his church and fully authorized messengers by means of preaching, the sacraments, and service. This salvation is due to the sacrificial crucifixion of Jesus Christ, which occurred once for all and for all mankind.

The appropriation of this salvation to individuals takes place first, however, through proclamation, which calls for decision, and through baptism, which places the believer in the service of love. Just as belief leads through repentance and baptism to eternal life, so unbelief leads through its rejection of the offer of salvation to damnation.

We therefore oppose the universalistic idea that in the crucifixion and resurrection of Jesus Christ all men of all times are already born again and already have peace with him, irrespective of their knowledge of the historical saving activity of God or belief in it. Through such a misconception the evangelizing commission loses both its full, authoritative power and its urgency. Unconverted men are thereby lulled into a fatal sense of security about their eternal destiny.

5   *But you are a chosen race, a royal priesthood, a dedicated nation, and a people claimed by God for his own, to proclaim the triumphs of him who has called you out of darkness into his marvelous light (I Pet. 2:9).*

     Adapt yourselves no longer to the pattern of this present world (Rom. 12:2).

We recognize and declare:

The primary visible task of mission is *to call out the messianic, saved community* from among all people.

Missionary proclamation should lead everywhere to the establishment of the Church of Jesus Christ, which exhibits a new, defined reality as salt and light in its social environment.

Through the Gospel and the sacraments, the Holy Spirit gives the members of the congregation a new life and an eternal, spiritual fellowship with each other and with God, who is real and present with them. It is the task of the congregation through its witness to move the lost—especially those who live outside its community—to a saving membership in the body of Christ. Only by being this new kind of fellowship does the Church present the Gospel convincingly.

We therefore oppose the view that the Church, as the fellowship of Jesus, is simply a part of the world. The contrast between the Church and the world is not merely a distinction in function and in knowledge of salvation; rather, it is an essential difference in nature. We deny that the Church has no advantage over the world except the knowledge of the alleged future salvation of all men.

We further oppose the one-sided emphasis on salvation which stresses only this world, according to which the Church and the world together share in a future, purely social, reconciliation of all mankind. That would lead to the self-dissolution of the Church.

6   *Remember then your former condition: . . . you were at that time separate from Christ, strangers to the community of Israel, outside God's cov-*

enants and the promise that goes with them. Your world was a world without hope and without God (Eph. 2:11, 12).

We recognize and declare:

The offer of salvation in Christ is directed without exception to all men who are not yet bound to him in conscious faith. The adherents to the nonchristian religions and world views can receive this salvation only through participation in faith. They must let themselves be freed from their former ties and false hopes in order to be admitted by belief and baptism into the body of Christ. Israel, too, will find salvation in turning to Jesus Christ.

We therefore reject the false teaching that the nonchristian religions and world views are also ways of salvation similar to belief in Christ.

We refute the idea that "Christian presence" among the adherents to the world religions and a give-and-take dialogue with them are substitutes for a proclamation of the Gospel which aims at conversion. Such dialogues simply establish good points of contact for missionary communication.

We also refute the claim that the borrowing of Christian ideas, hopes, and social procedures—even if they are separated from their exclusive relationship to the person of Jesus—can make the world religion and ideologies substitutes for the Church of Jesus Christ. In reality they give them a syncretistic and therefore antichristian direction.

7   *And this gospel of the kingdom will be proclaimed throughout the earth as a testimony to all nations; and then the end will come (Matt. 24:14).*

We recognize and declare:

The Christian world mission is the decisive, continuous saving activity of God among men between the time of the resurrection and second coming of Jesus Christ. Through the proclamation of the Gospel, new nations and people will progressively be called to decision for or against Christ.

When all people have heard the witness about him and have given their answer to it, the conflict between the Church of Jesus and the world, led by the Antichrist, will reach its climax. Then Christ himself will return and break into time, disarming the demonic power of Satan and establishing his own visible, boundless messianic kingdom.

We refute the unfounded idea that the eschatological expectation of the New Testament has been falsified by Christ's delay in returning and is therefore to be given up.

We refute at the same time the enthusiastic and utopian ideology that either under the influence of the Gospel or by the anonymous working of Christ in history, all of mankind is already moving toward a position of general peace and justice and will finally—before the return of Christ—be united under him in a great world community.

We refute the identification of messianic salvation with progress, development, and social change. The fatal consequence of this is that efforts to aid development and revolutionary involvement in the places of tension in society are seen as the contemporary forms of Christian mission. But such an identification would be a self-deliverance to the utopian movements of our time in the direction of their ultimate destination.

We do, however, affirm the determined advocacy of justice and peace by all churches, and we affirm that developmental aid is a timely realization of the divine demand for mercy and justice as well as of the command of Jesus "Love thy neighbor."

We see therein an important accompaniment and authentication of mission. We also affirm the humanizing results of conversion as signs of the coming messianic peace.

We stress, however, that unlike the eternally valid reconciliation with God through faith in the Gospel, all of our social achievements and partial successes in politics are restricted by the eschatological "not yet" of the coming kingdom and the not yet annihilated power of sin, death, and the devil, who still is the "prince of this world."

This establishes the priorities of our missionary service and causes us to extend ourselves in the expectation of Him who promises, "Behold! I make all things new" (Rev. 21:5, RSV).

622-1
5-39